A Memoir in Pieces

GRACE PERIOD

A MEMOIR IN PIECES

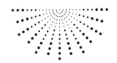

KELLY J. BAKER

Raven Books

Publisher's Cataloging-in-Publication Data
Baker, Kelly J. 1980-.
Grace Period: A Memoir in Pieces / Kelly J. Baker
p.____ cm.____
ISBN 978-1-947834-04-0 (Pbk.)
1. Education, Higher. 2. Women College Teachers. 3. Autobiography. I. Title.
814'.54—dc23 | 2017952960

Raven Books

Published by Raven Books
an imprint of Blue Crow Publishing, LLC
Chapel Hill, NC
www.bluecrowpublishing.com
Cover Photograph by Chris Baker
Cover Design by Lauren Faulkenberry

PRAISE FOR GRACE PERIOD: A MEMOIR IN
PIECES

Grace Period tracks the trials and triumphs of Baker's post-academic transition from 2013 to 2017 with great insight and humor. Baker deftly balances personal struggles and broad institutional inequities as she confronts the trauma of leaving the academy. Recounting the many miseries of applying, adjuncting, interviews, rejection, writing, book contracts, disappearing jobs, and a certain disciplinary task force on contingency, Baker makes her way to the personal turning point, smack in the middle of the book: "I'm no longer transitioning away from academic work and life. I'm moving forward, one small step at a time." Her journey will help many traverse their own paths forward.

— KAREN KELSKY, PH.D., THE AUTHOR
OF THE PROFESSOR IS IN: THE
ESSENTIAL GUIDE TO TURNING YOUR
PH.D. INTO A JOB

In a series of vivid and beautiful essays, Baker uses her changing relationship to academia to reflect on "grace periods," those moments (or strings of moments) when you leave one possible future behind without quite knowing what's next.

— DEREK ATTIG, PH.D., BOOK RIOT

CONTENTS

ALSO BY KELLY J. BAKER

Gospel According to the Klan: The KKK's Appeal to Protestant America, 1915-1930

The Zombies Are Coming! The Realities of the Zombie Apocalypse in American Culture

To Chris

INTRODUCTION

In January 2012, I was riding in the backseat next to our three-year-old, Kara, as my partner, Chris, drove. We had just celebrated Christmas with our families in Florida. We had an eight-and-a-half-hour drive from Florida back to Tennessee. I picked up my phone to pass the time and instead found out that an academic, in my own subfield, committed suicide. I didn't know this scholar. I had heard of their work in passing, but I found myself reading a blog post written by one of their friends lamenting the sharp, painful loss of a dear friend. By all accounts, this scholar was a talented historian, who likely applied for the same few jobs that I applied for in the same disastrous job market that kept me sleepless for more nights than I was willing to admit. I couldn't know what led to the end of this scholar's life. But, I wondered about what role the job market played. And I hated myself for wondering.

When we stopped to fill up the tank in northern Georgia, my mind was focused on the tragedy of a stranger instead of where I should put my feet. I stepped over a gas line with one foot and tripped over it with the other. Before I knew what was happening, I landed hard on the pavement. My left arm endured most of the impact. The bone snapped close to my elbow, though I didn't realize it then. I knew something was wrong because of the pain, but I insisted that Chris keep driving rather than head to a nearby hospital. I wanted to go home. The pressure of the holidays and the questions about my job search already worked me over. My arm throbbing in pain wouldn't keep me from returning to the car and pleading with Chris to *just drive.* I draped my arm across my chest, and my eyes leaked tears for the rest of the drive.

All I could think of was whether my arm was truly injured, broken even, and how that might impact the potential job interviews I hoped to have in the spring. I managed to break my arm, and all I could think about was my academic career. My thoughts returned to the impossibility of the job market in the humanities and to the death of someone I never knew. It was hard to breathe as my arm throbbed. Could that have been me? No, yes, no, I wasn't sure.

I thought about what the academic life was *worth* to me. I had been on the job market for years. I had gotten conference interviews and campus visits, but no job offers. As I applied year in and year out, I adjuncted in New Mexico and then in Tennessee. I had a kid and revised my dissertation into a book. The cycle of the academic job market defined my life: the possibility of potential jobs appearing in the early fall, the winnowing of that potential with every position that I didn't receive a conference interview, and the profound disappointment of the spring when yet again no job appeared.

As I tried not to shift my injured arm, I couldn't help but think about how academia claimed my life. How had it become the *entirety* of my life? *No*, I told myself, *it couldn't be my whole life, could it?* I hoped not. The more I pondered how academia affected every aspect of my life, the more distraught I became. I had a partner, a daughter, two dogs, and a remarkably evil kitty. I was a daughter, sister, mother, partner, and friend too, but those roles seemed curtailed by my scholarship and my unending job hunt. My life was more than my academic work, right? But, I also couldn't imagine what my life would be if I wasn't an academic. Was there a life I could build outside of a career that took years of training and structured my life semester by semester? What would I be if I weren't an American religious historian? What would I be if I weren't an academic?

What I was afraid to even consider was whether I wanted the life I tried so desperately to create. Whether I wanted different opportunities and possibilities. Whether the academic life was one that I wanted rather than what other people, like my advisor and other faculty, thought I should have. Whether I should have I followed their lead instead of imagining another path.

By the next day, when an x-ray confirmed that I managed to break my arm and would be wearing a sling for months, I brushed aside those concerns about academic life. Surely, that was the pain talking. But, the doubt about my path lingered. I couldn't quite shake the feeling that I was rushing toward a life that didn't really want me.

Only a year later, I realized that I had had enough. Another round on the job market ended in a bust. One job that I applied for, an open-rank professorship, had 900 applicants. I made it to the short list of 12 candidates for phone interviews, but I didn't make the cut for campus visits.

A colleague told me that I should stay on the job market just one more year because I was such a "strong" candidate. She meant well. But as she assured me that I needed to give my job search a little more time, just another year, I realized that I couldn't do it anymore. I couldn't stand another year of applying for all the jobs that I wouldn't get. I couldn't take one more rejection. I couldn't go through another cycle of possibility and crushed dreams.

Months went by, and I wasn't sure what to do beyond teach my classes, spend time with my family, and stay afloat.

At the same time that I was fed up with my job search, Chris was increasingly unhappy about his job at the national lab. He received a job offer to work for a tech start-up and jumped at the chance. We could live anywhere because the company allowed telecommuting. Our second child was due in September, so we decided to move to Florida to be closer to our families. He decided to leave academia behind; I decided to take a break to figure out my options.

In April 2013, I wrote a post, "Not a Real Academic," based on Twitter interactions I had with a few others about academia. I didn't intend for the piece to be anything other than an outlet for my frustrations. And yet, people read it. More than that, the essay resonated. A month later, I wrote "Grace Period" to let people (friends, family, colleagues, students, and the random readers of my site) that I was taking a year off to figure out what to do with my life. I wanted folks to know that I had quit my job as a lecturer and moved to Florida, and I didn't want to send countless emails explaining myself. Someone kindly pointed out that post to the editors of *The Chronicle of Higher Education*'s new project, *Vitae*.

While in the hospital after the birth of my son, I received an email from one of their editors offering me the opportunity to write about my transition out of academia. In a haze of no sleep and brand-new baby, I wasn't sure whether to accept or not, but I did anyway. So, I started writing about my year off and my transition out of academia. "Grace Period" became a series by accident. I never thought that essay would amount to much, but I wrote one essay and another and another and another. Essay by essay, I chronicled how my year off turned into two years. I cataloged how I felt about what I left behind and what was hopefully in front of me. I ended the series on *Vitae* with "Goodbye to All That," but I still kept writing in the vein of "Grace Period" (for *Vitae*, on my blog, and in my TinyLetter) about how I felt about my transition. I couldn't quite give up the series, even after I claimed it was over. And surprisingly, readers followed my journey. They read my essays at *Vitae*. They subscribed to my TinyLetter. They emailed and tweeted me their own experiences and transitions.

I decided to collect all the essays together, so that they all finally could rest side-by-side. You can see my journey from beginning to a sort of ending, so you can realize that transitions are hard, oh-so-hard, but we can make it through them. Hopefully, you can realize, like I did, that lives can be built outside the academy (and other institutions), if only we start to imagine alternatives.

Realizing there's something beyond the paths that we work and bleed to create is the first step. As Cheryl Strayed reminds us, "You don't have a career. You have a life."[1]

The essays that follow were my attempts to build and rebuild my life. There's a vulnerability to these essays that I didn't recognize while writing them. Some are heartbreaking. It still hurts to read them now three years later. Others are hopeful, and they reassured me when I wasn't always hopeful. My hope is that these essays will make you, dear reader, hopeful too. We don't know how our lives will turn out, no matter how much we plan, scheme, strategize, and fight for control. There's a freedom in the not knowing. It just took me a long time to realize it. I hope you can too.

April 2017

———

1. Cheryl Strayed, "Dear Sugar, The Rumpus Advice Column #64: Tiny Beautiful Things," *The Rumpus*, February 10, 2011.

1

NOT A REAL ACADEMIC

A few years ago, I was at a graduate conference presenting on a panel on post-graduate life. I was the "part-time" panelist, the one who had not secured the vaunted tenure-track job but was adjuncting at a big state university. When I wasn't teaching, I was in charge of my toddler. On the drive to and from the university, I dreamed of seeking some sort of balance between home life and career. As I drove back and forth, I mulled my life decisions. I agonized over my choices, but I realized that I wouldn't have made different ones. More importantly, I couldn't imagine putting my career before my partner and child, and I still can't. That's my decision, and it will always be my most important one.

Perhaps, I was not the best panelist to discuss the life of the post-grad. I pretty much lacked sleep because of my anxiety about doing everything wrong: work, life, and especially motherhood. Doubt was a constant companion, but so was the naïve hope about the job market. I was waiting for my *moment* when all of the trauma would be washed away by THE JOB, the tenure-track position that I had been trained for. Sure, the job market turned south, but surely, I could find a job, right? My book was coming out, and I had several articles coming soon. My advisor suggested that I was a strong candidate, and my CV made me a contender. My mantra became "just a little more time and things will work out." Things work out for others, so why not for me? I still had hope at this point.

All of this is to say that my talk for the panel stumped me. I wasn't entirely sure what to say to graduate students. "Just hang in there" seemed like a silly platitude even then. "You'll all get jobs" was a lie I refused to utter. "If you dream it, you can do it" made me want to hurl. "Just work hard" ignored the structural constraints of the modern university. I really was a terrible choice, if the audience craved inspiration.

I wanted to communicate all of my struggles and frustrations. I wanted to tell them that adjuncting sucks because of low pay, bad schedules, and little prestige. I wanted to scream that the research career that I trained for was only possible because I arrived at my office by 6 a.m. on my "teaching days" or because I worked furiously during naptime. I wanted to point out that teaching is truly undervalued; my department head once told me to give students "less" than I thought they needed because students don't need "much" followed by a remark on using my time wisely rather than on my teaching, which I should emphasize was *my job*. I wanted to explain that the only reason I could live off adjuncting is because I have a partner who works and supports me. I wanted to share that being on the job market made me physically ill and mentally weary. I wanted to say that maybe this academic life was not for me. Maybe, I wasn't cut out for it.

I would find myself looking into the mirror and wondering why I wanted to have *this* career so badly. Were the costs worth it? I wanted to be honest. And I mostly was. One of my mentors told me I couldn't be completely honest because the graduate students would flee. This comment stunned me, and it made it very hard from me to sleep the night before the panel. What was I supposed to do? Maybe, I should encourage fleeing. Maybe not, but maybe so.

As I sat outside in the sunshine before my Sunday morning panel, I read over my notes for my talk. I still struggled with what to say. One of my best friends from graduate school, who decided not to pursue an academic career, was also on the panel. She loved her job, and she seemed happy. I was envious of her bravery to leave it all behind; I was equally nervous about what my envy said about me.

I turned again to my scribbled notes: What to say about the academy and post-graduate life?

As my friend and I were walking into the conference, I encountered a professor who I knew casually but was outside my own subfield. We chatted amiably about the panel. Then, things took a turn. I am not sure how it happened because memory fails me. Somehow, I mentioned my insecurity about my position as a part-time academic. He responded by telling me that I couldn't be a "real" academic until I had a tenure-track job. It took me a moment to process what he had said because I couldn't believe someone would actually utter such a thing aloud. Sure, this is the way the story is told. The winners get tenure-track jobs, and the rest of us did something wrong. He struck me as someone who believed in fabled meritocracy and ignored that tenure-track jobs were becoming a rarity. He was lucky that I didn't give into my urge to punch him. Hard.

It was as if what I feared had come to life. My demons confronted me in the Florida sunshine in the form of a well-meaning but clueless white dude. Somehow all the effort and agony did not matter because I wasn't "real." My work did not have some elusive stamp of approval. All of it was for naught. What the hell was I supposed to say to students now? *Please ignore me as I contemplate my lack of reality? Don't listen to me because I don't matter?* Instead of falling into despair, I got angry and gave my talk anyway.

But, his comment still lingers with me. I've given it too much power and weight. I still wonder if I am a "real" academic, but mostly, I am not sure that I want to be judged by someone else's standards of who an academic is or can be. Some days, I want to walk away for good rather than just taking a year off. Is there really anything I will miss? Other days, I find myself caught up in my research and writing. I like what I do. Yet, that still feels as if it is not enough to make me stay, but it might be enough to make me go.

What happens if I remake the "real" and the "academic" to suit my standards? What if I embrace that I don't want to be what my training suggests is valuable, successful, or correct? What if I just say the hell with it?

Just a little more time, I tell myself, *things will work out.* Won't they?

JULY 2013

GRACE PERIOD

In May, I quit my job and moved to Florida. Both decisions might seem big (they were), but they were remarkably easy. My lecturer gig paid little, the teaching load was heavy, and my department was dysfunctional. Leaving behind students, friends, and colleagues was hard. Watching my daughter mourn the loss of her friends was harder.

The move to Florida was unexpected. Out of the blue, Chris was offered a new job with a tech company, which allowed him to telecommute. To my surprise, he took the job, and we decided to move to Florida to be closer to our families. We both walked away from academia, the careers we trained for. That surprised us both. He might go back. I find myself more ambivalent.

Except, I didn't walk away. Not really. Instead, I embraced a safer option, a year hiatus from the academy. *Reassess and figure things out*, I tell myself, *decide whether to stay or not*. Delay the inevitable is probably more likely. It's more like a grace period (maybe). Am I going to pay my "debt" to my academic training?

Or am I going to do something, anything, else? What I know is that now I have time to breathe, to reflect, to dream, to recreate, and to mourn. I can decide if there is anything that I will miss about academic life. I can decide to take the parts I like (research and writing) and apply them to other careers. I can decide to walk away. The choice, for once, rests on my shoulders.

After five years on the job market, I found myself burned out. I've had conference interviews and campus visits. I've been a second choice for tenure-track jobs multiple times. I applied for jobs while teaching three and four classes a semester. And I finished my first book, wrote articles and book reviews, received a contract for a new book, edited a journal, organized panels, and experimented with an e-book. *The harder I worked*, I thought naïvely, *the more likely I was to get a job*. Optimism is a hard habit to kick.

During this past spring semester, something broke. My tireless drive to research and write dissipated. The latest round of rejections hit harder than previous rounds, and I was tired. Why make myself get up extra early to write if there was no tenure-track job for me? Why spend the time researching when I would rather spend time with my daughter? Why kill myself for a job opportunity that would never materialize? I found that I couldn't do the work I used to love. My motivation stalled. Something broke, and it seemed irreparable.

This was compounded by my increasing frustration with my job as a lecturer. I liked my students, I enjoyed teaching, and I despised the undervaluing of teaching by my department head. I disliked the hierarchy of talents, in which tenure-track and tenured faculty were valued more than those of us who "just" taught. Being a lecturer meant that my publications could be brushed aside, and that my experience and opinions mattered less. Frustrating doesn't quite cover it.

The desire to throw up my hands and walk away chased me through the day. There must be more to academic life than this. I hoped for something that would make my training and efforts redeemable, and I struggled to find it. Why should I stay? That thought is a dangerous one. Once it roots, nothing makes it disappear. It remains and confronts. It pounces on me in Florida now as I try to figure out what I am going to do next.

I mourn what my career could have been, and I struggle to redefine who I am now. Doubt, my old friend, bubbles to the surface as I ponder what I could do alongside what it is possible to do. The grace period is simultaneously too long and too short. Is it a transition? A re-evaluation? A transformation? Is this a shedding of one vision of self to become a better version? Is it a loss of dreams? Is it a moment to dwell in the liminal?

Most days, it is hard to tell. But, I find myself mourning less as days go by. The loss of what could have been is less suffocating and distracting. A transition feels manageable and desirable. The possibilities for what could be are more and more exciting. I might not be an academic after my grace period, and that's okay. I am more than my training. And so are all of you. It is best to never forget that.

NOVEMBER 2013

HOW TO (NOT) AVOID THE JOB MARKET

When I decided to take a year away from academia, one of my goals was to avoid the job market. For five years, fall was a time of anticipation and dread as I waited to see what jobs would be available. How many jobs this year? How many could I apply for? What were the application requirements? How would I balance teaching, research, and job applications? How much would I despise myself after I had all the rejections in hand?

I hated job season, but I couldn't really hate it either. The drudgery of compiling applications, and the critical self-scrutiny that accompanied it, were tiresome, but applying was the only way to get an elusive tenure-track job. Thus, I prepared for the market by crafting (and recrafting) research and teaching statements, updating my CV, and writing letters for each position. These tasks took much time and effort.

Yet the most painful part of the process was asking recommenders for letters year after year. I tried to act confident and self-assured when I politely requested letters (again) and graciously accepted their assurances that this year (unlike other years) would be my year. I even garnered enough optimism to halfway believe them. That optimism required equal parts hope and delusion, and to muster those simultaneously took exhaustive amounts of mental and physical energy, without which I might not have applied to any jobs. With them, I faced sleepless nights and gut-wrenching anxiety. Hope and delusion pulled me through multiple job cycles. This cycle, however, was different because I was not "on the market." I'd opted out.

When this fall rolled around, I felt no trepidation. I had no need to gird my optimism and stave off my anxiety. I did not have to look obsessively at the American Academy of Religion's jobs site to see which new ads were posted. I did not frantically search the H-Net job guide for some position that might be a good fit. I did not need to strategize with mentors about how best to showcase my talents to search committees.

More importantly, I did not have to talk about the market and why I still hadn't secured a tenure-track job. In previous years, discussions about why I had not been placed were always torturous. The blame generally fell on me as an individual, as if I were somehow solely in control of my destiny. These discussions often skirted the structural constraints of modern universities and the whims of search committees.

This year, I knew that I could avoid all of that because I was avoiding the job market. Out of sight, out of mind. Or so I thought. The funny thing, of course, is that the beast we call the job market does not care about my grievances or my attempts to ignore it. It carries on without me and claims other victims. I soon realized the naïveté in my strategy: you can't expect everyone to go along with you.

My first brush with the job market came on Twitter. Colleagues tweeted about jobs at their institutions, with links to the postings and fun commentary about joining their departments. I clicked the links. Some of these jobs seemed like a good fit. *If only this job had been available last year*, I thought, *maybe I would have had a chance*. Doubts claimed me. Should I apply? These moments of weakness led me to panic. What if one of these jobs was *the job*? What if I tanked my own career by sitting out this job cycle?

My panic turned to terror as I questioned my decision to take a year off. What if I was making an irreparable mistake? The "what ifs" plagued me.

Then I started receiving emails asking me to forward job announcements to whomever might be interested. And then my Facebook friends started posting about jobs they were applying for and the stress of completing applications. Everywhere I turned, the market was present. It was stalking me on social media and in conversations with friends. It was haunting me in every tweet, status update, and coffee date.

So, I decided to fight back. I tweeted about my anxiety and my fear, and I messaged friends who'd made similar decisions. The support I received was overwhelming. Colleagues and friends in both academic and alt-ac careers encouraged me to stick to my original plan of not applying. They shared stories about their own decisions to opt out of the market and affirmed the difficulty of those decisions. They told me why they chose the paths they did, and what those paths had cost. Their honesty reaffirmed my desire to take the year to figure things out.

Crucially, this made me confront my true fears: relinquishing my academic career and abandoning my optimism. This choice to opt out suggested that I was no longer a researcher and a teacher. Sometimes I feel like I am giving up an important part of myself. My anxiety about the job market was my anxiety about who I wanted to be slammed up against the realities of who I could be.

What I realize now is that my expectations about who I want to be have shifted. The market no longer has me in its grip because I am unsure whether I want what it has to offer. It can't haunt me anymore, but I must reckon with its presence. Avoidance hasn't worked, because now I have to confront a different truth. I no longer want a tenure-track job, so where do I go from here?

DECEMBER 2013

4

THE HARD BUSINESS OF LETTING GO

"a kind of goodbye to all that, to all this—to this person I imagined myself as or imagined I'd become, this identity that I needed so badly in order to feel good about myself."

— LAUREN QUINN

"Where do I go from here, how do I proceed now without goal, without path: how do I float?"

— SARAH MENKEDICK

I search job ads at local universities. Obsessively. I started this as soon as we moved to Florida. Perusing the ads was a way to figure out alternate paths. It (supposedly) gave me a feel for what kinds of jobs were available. I avoided faculty and adjunct listings, focusing instead on administrative positions.

Perhaps, I thought, I could stay in higher education in a different capacity.

Relentless perusal, I assured myself, *was for the best.* My grace period will eventually end. I'll need to know what kinds of jobs are available. "It's just research," I say aloud. My infant son gurgles at me skeptically. Chris and I talk about possible career options; we strategize about turning my CV into a resume. I tell him that maybe the perfect job will come along. He nods supportively. I smile tentatively.

In early November, an academic-advisor position becomes available at a nearby university. It requires working with student athletes, which I've done before and enjoyed. The job is one that I've already considered as a good fit. I read and reread the job description, imagining how I might sell myself to the hiring manager. I might even love a job like this.

The pros and cons of the advisor position seem pretty clear. It's a mostly 9-to-5 job, and my schedule would lack some of flexibility that I was used to in my previous lectureship. Both my five-year-old daughter and my infant son would have to go into full-time daycare, costing a whopping $1,400 a month. There would be no summers off, and I would spend less time with my children. There would also be little time to finish my manuscript, which is under contract.

Yet I am excited about the prospect of working with students again. I miss students and teaching more than I thought I would. *Maybe I can find a place for myself at a university without being contingent labor,* I think. Maybe I can be happy with this as my career. Maybe I should take the plunge and reinvent myself on the alt-ac track.

As the deadline looms, the cons seem to outweigh the pros. The daycare costs alone give me pause. Downgrading my writing and research to hobbies bothers me more than I expect. The decision to apply feels rushed. Why am I jumping so quickly at this opportunity? Wasn't I was supposed to take the year off? Why am I pressuring myself to apply? The internal pressure subsumes me. It paralyzes me.

The deadline passes. I don't apply for the job. Self-scrutiny remains.

Guilt rears its ugly head. I had let an opportunity pass me by. How very unlike me! I feel unmoored and cowardly. The only way to move on from academia was to move on. Make choices. Apply for jobs. Be fearless. Experiment with new possibilities. Instead, I stalled. What happened to that fearless and confident woman that I was before graduate school and the job market? When did I lose her? How can I get her back? What would she think of me now? Would my 22-year-old self be disappointed in her 33-year-old counterpart?

Realization punches me in the gut. That woman was long gone. She dissipated with every year. She became less fearless, more nervous. My dream to become a professor floated away, too, in the flurry of applications and the brutal realities of the job market. The career that I trained for appears more and more untenable day by day.

Applying for a job off the tenure-track, then, felt like the death knell of my dream. I stalled, not because I am a coward, but because abandoning who you think you are going to be is hard. I've let the dream I haven't achieved define me more than my accomplishments. That dream turned toxic, and it is time to let it go.

This realization hovered over me from the moment I decided to take a year off. I've been struggling to ignore it. I have to let go, and now, I'm ready.

I get to find a new dream—or dreams. I get to figure out who I want to be. I get to be fearless again.

JANUARY 2014

————

1. Lauren Quinn, "Goodbye to All of This," *Vela Magazine*, November 13, 2013.
2. Sarah Menkedick, "Learning to Float," *Vela Magazine*, November 20, 2013.

5
(NON)TOXIC DREAMS

Writing "The Hard Business of Letting Go" proved more emotional than my other essays. Dwelling on what it is like to realize that a dream is dead and gone with no real hope of resurrection was harder than I expected. What happens when you are forced to let go and move on? How do you feel when you confront that searing truth? What if you no longer recognize yourself?

It hurts to write about owning up to the fact that my career won't be what I imagined. I have to find new dreams. The end. On to the next column.

But, an interesting thing happened when I posted this particular essay on Facebook. One of my mentors and dear friend, Martin Kavka, asked me, "Are there such things as non-toxic dreams?" His question stunned me. He continued:

> I ask in some seriousness, and with a lot of trepidation. I ask in seriousness because I suspect that the contingency of life

means that all dreams will always be crushed. I ask with trepidation because I fear that my suspicion ends up functioning only as a way to occlude all the structural problems of academia...Are there such things as non-toxic dreams?

Academia was my dream, but lately, I'm not sure that I was ever really suited for it. The pursuit of an academic career turned me into a strange, neurotic woman, whom I avoided in the mirror. Frantic, busy, tired, anxious, irritable, pessimistic, and depressed. I mastered my brave, public face. It appeared as if nothing bothered me, but everything did.

When I decided to take a year off, I sort of fell apart. I cut and dyed my hair over and over, as if changing my appearance would somehow change my life. As if making myself look different meant I was no longer myself. As if I could change myself into someone different with a little hair dye and a new attitude. As if I could escape myself if I only kept trying to.

I vacillated between anger and sadness. Slowly, I started to feel better, as I realized that my failure as an academic had very little to do with me and mostly with the labor structure of the university. Most days I'm happy with my decision to move on. Some days I'm still miserable. This dream was clearly toxic, and the aftereffects still linger and plague me.

So, are there such things as non-toxic dreams? Martin's words stick with me as I try to find my place out of academia and in this world. I turn the question around: Are all dreams inherently toxic? The bleakness of the inversion makes me catch my breath. I pause. I have no words. *Please don't let that be true,*

I utter. What are we left with if things that we want to sustain us actually harm us? What are we to do if our dreams will always cause us pain?

The cynical part of me finds truth in toxicity. What if all dreams are eroded by what Lauren Berlant calls the "wearying" of life in *Cruel Optimism*? For Berlant, the mundane sleights of the everyday are more damaging than those big, shocking events called "trauma." Drudgery and repetition eat away at us day in and day out. We cannot escape them. We are weary; I am weary. Life is weary-making. Berlant warns us of the fantasies of the good life that seem to dominate American culture. The good life is elusive, if not impossible. Optimism most often turns cruel. Positive visions of the future might damn us, more than they ever save us.

I find this compelling and disquieting. Berlant challenges the ubiquitous "life is good" t-shirts in cheery, pastel colors. T-shirt wisdom should never be trusted. After all, life is hard. People reach for this mantra when confronted with the suffering of others. *Life is hard for everyone*, they say, *why would academia be any different?* We suffer, so why should we be surprised that you suffer too?

They are right. Life is hard and fragile and fleeting. That brusque statement of fact, however, is not an excuse to ignore structural injustices wherever they may be. We can't use "life is hard" to obscure the pain and suffering of others, inside or outside academia. This oft-repeated sentiment does not absolve the complexity or particularity of the "hard." The wearying of the world impacts each of us. Life is hard both systemically and individually. To admit that life is hard is the beginning of a conversation, not an end. To use it as an explanatory end is a callous approach to those around us. It's cruelty rather than kindness.

We can no longer ignore that the dream of a tenure-track job is most often fantasy rather than reality. Adjuntification is the new normal. Optimism becomes cruel in every advisor's assurance to students that they will get secure jobs. Toxicity blooms noxious and thick. It smothers and chokes us. Letting go of that dream, for me, is the only way to live.

Yet, I can't give up dreaming. I'm an idealist, who hopes fervently that some dreams are less toxic. Maybe, some dreams nourish. I need to dream, so the wearying does not overwhelm me. Berlant might call me a stupid optimist; I'm okay with that. I refuse to quit dreaming even if that means that new dreams could turn on me. That's a chance I have to take.

Are there such things as non-toxic dreams? Let's find out.

JANUARY 2014

6

THE IMPERMANENT ADJUNCT

As my year off moves by slowly, I often wonder how I arrived at the situation I am in. Was there a pivotal moment that set me on this path? When did I begin to doubt that I would ever fit neatly within the academy? When did quitting become an inevitability rather than a possibility? There's one answer to all these questions: *when I became a contingent laborer.*

I never planned to have a temporary job. I fell into one, as people often do. While finishing my dissertation out of residence, I started adjuncting. I moved with my husband to a place 23 hours from home for his *paid* internship (which eventually turned into a *paid* postdoc). I was lonely and isolated. My cohort was far away, as were my other friends and family. I missed teaching—in my graduate program, we taught early and often—and I craved familiarity. Adjuncting put me back in the classroom, and it was (supposedly) a way to avoid the dreaded gap on my CV.

I ended up adjuncting at a community college and a university simultaneously. At the university, the pay per course was about $1,500, with a promise of $1,800 when I finished my Ph.D. At the community college, the pay was less, and I had no control over curriculum or books. This 20th-century Americanist ended up teaching Early World Civilizations.

Most fall and spring semesters, I taught two courses for the community college and one for the university. In my second-to-last semester, pregnant and finishing my dissertation, I taught a total of five classes between three campuses. I had agreed to teach only four courses, but at the forceful cajoling of an administrator, I took over one more.

An adjunct-turned-professor had broken her leg in a nasty fall, the administrator said; she had become immobile. She had been adjuncting at the community college for at least 20 years—maybe even as many as 25 (I can't remember the exact number)—and she had finally moved into a tenure-track position just the semester before. The injury forced her to retire early. Can you imagine years and years of adjuncting coalescing at last into an elusive tenure-track position, only to be taken away by slippery snow and unsteady feet? Fate is more often cruel than kind.

This was the beginning of my life as a contingent laborer, and I was blissfully unaware of it. Like many graduate students, I assumed that adjuncting was a pit stop. I would go on the job market and earn a tenure-track job, because that's what happened to good students (or so I had been told). When I broached jobs with my advisor and committee members, they assured me that I would have no trouble getting a job. They seemed to be right since I was invited to four campus visits for assistant-professor jobs in 2008. During one visit, I was told that I would be an excellent diversity hire, because the department of almost all white men needed "at least one" white woman.

What I soon realized is that I had no problem getting a job teaching as an adjunct or, later, as a full-time, non-tenure-track faculty member. The problem was finding a permanent position rather than a contingent one. Maybe I should have been more specific in my queries to my advisors and mentors.

We moved again in September 2009 for Chris's new job. (Computational-science Ph.D.'s are more employable than religious-studies Ph.D.'s, if you didnt already know this.) I started adjuncting again in January 2010 as a fill-in for a religious studies faculty member on leave. I taught part-time on Mondays, Wednesdays, and Fridays not only in religious studies, but also in American studies. I juggled part-time teaching with child care. Part-time often felt like full-time.

The American Studies department bungled my paperwork, so I wasn't paid for my course until almost the end of term. This happened not once, but twice. The head of the department apologized profusely. *How could this happen?* he mumbled when I confronted him about it. *You'll be okay until the money comes through, right?* I pasted on a smile and assured him that I would be. In my car on the way home, I cried. My husband's salary covered us, but I felt like a failure. I couldn't even get paid my paltry salary on time. We had rearranged our family's life for this part-time gig, so my husband or I could watch our daughter when the other was working. And I couldn't even get paid for my labor.

Yet, I kept doing part-time work semester by semester. I

wanted some connection with the university and some form of employment for my CV. I naïvely hoped that being a good department member would lead to a tenure-track job in religious studies. (American Studies was a program with no permanent faculty, so it was a lost cause.) So I did extra, unpaid work to show my willingness to be a team player. I attended evening events, worked with the undergrad majors in their religious-studies association, and volunteered to help out wherever I could. This was a small department with more lecturers than tenure-track and tenured faculty. There was always something to be done.

The department head even instituted "voluntary" service for lecturers, so we could improve our "portfolios" for the job market. Each lecturer was basically assigned a service task. While we were technically *asked* to do service, how could we turn it down? The head assigned all contracts for lecturers and had the sole power to revoke them. Saying "no" could have jeopardized our employment, so we did the work—even though all lecturers are on a teaching contract with no service requirements. More labor and no pay.

Still, I felt like I couldn't complain too much. I had a job when many didn't. I had an office (though I was moved three times). Most of my colleagues treated me with respect. A new assistant professor did ask me to make his copies as a joke; I didn't find this funny. I had some control over my schedule, thanks to the new associate head, who factored in my daughter's daycare. I received some funding to go to conferences.

Yet my job was not fully secure, and this bothered me. Each

semester I hoped that the department's budget would allow me to continue to work for $4,000 a class. I feared that I might be replaced by someone else. I clung to this job because at least it *was* a job.

Eventually, I transitioned from part-time to full-time with a yearlong contract. A modicum of stability came with a heavier teaching load. I was employed for the whole year, but anxiety loomed when it came time for my contract to be renewed.

I duped myself into believing that I needed to stay in that tenuous position, so I endured the indignities of being an "irregular" faculty member (the "regular" faculty were tenured and tenure-track). When I missed a meeting of the seminar designed by a senior faculty member, he complained to the head. The next day she scolded me in the hallway about my absence and told me that I must attend so as to not hurt his feelings. To avoid missing the seminar, I rearranged my teaching schedule. This is just one example of many I could offer.

My contingent status meant I was treated as *just* a lecturer, but called on to be so much more. I was expected to act as a fully invested member of a department that didn't seem to want me on its permanent roster. I was supposed to be loyal to an institution that was not loyal to me.

Here's the thing about being a contingent worker: Life begins to feel contingent too. I could never truly settle down because my job could disappear with the new budget cycle. Making long-term plans seemed fruitless because my situation was unstable. My life was stalled. I was not moving backward, but there was no forward motion either. The gears were gummed up. I felt like I was in a tedious holding pattern and I might stay there forever.

I couldn't live this way, so I stopped. And now? If a contingent position is my only option, I doubt I'll ever return to academia. Maybe this is why quitting feels inevitable.

FEBRUARY 2014

7

I'M OVER MY DISCIPLINE

As I was driving recently, a thought struck me. (Most of my self-revelations come while driving, if you were curious.) I realized that I'm over my sub-discipline, American religious history.

I said it aloud to see how the words would feel tumbling out of my mouth. *I'm over American religious history*, I recited again and again. It felt liberating, strange, and significant. I was once so passionate about my field. Now, as my emotions cooled, I felt disinterested and aloof. *Over it*, I said again as if to cement my feelings. *Over it*, I chanted. I wasn't sure I believed myself.

After all, I've dedicated years to the study of religions in America. That's quite a commitment to abandon on a revelatory whim. Have I really lost interest? Do I no longer want to be an American religious historian? Does how I identify myself matter that much? (Yes.) Letting go seems to require a hard break that cleaves off my former academic self. This break might be the only way to make room for a new self, unburdened by the baggage of my training. (Do I want to be unburdened?) Forgetting who I was might be the easiest way to become someone new.

If only transitions could be so simple. I can't entirely let go of something I once loved because love has everything to do with it.

I fell in love with American religions as an undergraduate. I majored in American studies, a jack-of-all-trades discipline that required few core courses at my university. I floated from discipline to discipline, trying to find something that captivated me: art history, American history, public administration, and religious studies. The latter caught my attention, and after a few courses, I fell hard. This newfound love guided me into graduate school. Love and graduate school go hand-in-hand.[1]

I both adored and loathed my training. I see-sawed from romantic highs (seminar discussions, research, theory) to tortured lows (self-doubt, impostor syndrome, research). I almost quit multiple times. Yet I trudged through, because love is about compromise, or so they say.

It took me a long while to figure out that what I was compromising might be too much to bear. Fragments of me dissipated with every passing year of graduate training. Love rarely lifted me, but it often wounded me. Academia appeared as a bad boyfriend or a "bloody valentine."[2] I was caught in a bad romance.

Like all love, this love was, at its best, ambivalent. If only it had been fully terrible, my decisions would have been different. But it was frequently exhilarating. I binged on my field. I had academic crushes. I had fun debating colleagues and writing paper after paper. I eagerly awaited new monographs and cleared precious hours to read them. My marginalia would chase up and down the outer edges of their pages—love notes to the field tucked away in every book. Some works inspired me; others made me angry.

My anger often brought into focus the taut boundaries of my discipline. After all, my research was on an "unloved" group —white supremacists, who make scholars and general audiences uncomfortable, nervous, and often hostile. Who cares about them? Should you care about them? Through much of my early dissertation research, I felt crushingly alone. It seemed that no one else was interested in the research problems that consumed me. It was a solitary, unappreciated love, which made it fierce and unrelenting.

Later, I found colleagues who emerged as a support group of mutual affect. Our passion drove us to reexamine and critique our field. My emotions were deeply invested not only in my own scholarship, but also in the currents of the discipline. Yet my attention, my attraction, changed. I was still passionate about the identity of American religions, but I wanted the discipline to change to become better. I wanted to fix my romance. This was the beginning of the end.

This love was tainted from the start; it always contained sorrow. Love is never just about joy, pleasure, or affirmation. Reciprocity is never guaranteed. And academic love is inherently one-sided. I could love my field without reservation, but the field could never really love me back. That's the danger of investing wholeheartedly in any work; the return never matches the devotion. This love is sacrificial and rarely redemptive. The price it extracts is too high. It breaks our hearts into sharp, pained pieces. Love, like optimism, can turn cruel.

We get hurt by academia because of our love, not in spite of it. "Quit lit," after all, is about heartbreak.[3] We quit in a rush of words to communicate our pain. We break up with academia, institutions, and our fields. Academic love echoes romantic love, and sometimes they both end badly. And the expectation that we'll desperately love our work, as Miya Tokumitsu points out, allows us to be exploited.[4]

And here's the problem: Exploitation doesn't make us love our work less. Instead, it often pushes us to love that work more —to consider it something deeper, a vocation instead of just a job. I clung more tightly to academic love at the low points of my career, as if all I needed was love to remedy my situation. *Don't love*, they tell us. *It is just a job*, they say. But this ignores that many of us already have the gossamer hooks of love anchored in our flesh.

Even now, as I can admit that I no longer feel that strongly about my field, the language of love still manages to inundate me. Friends and colleagues keep telling me that I love my work too much to leave. They can't imagine me abandoning my work. They email to say that my discipline needs me. They tell me that they miss our conversations. They worry that I'm going to walk away. Didn't I love being an academic? Yes, I did. Wasn't I passionate about my research? Yes, I was. What will the field do without me? It'll move along. While I might have once loved it, the field cares not for me.

It hurts to leave my discipline, but it hurts even more to stay. Goodbye, American religious history. It's me, not you. Sort of.

Over coffee, I tell a friend about my breakup with the field. My confession feels unwieldy and weighty. I'm nervous about her reaction. She smiles and responds that my questions are bigger than the field. They always have been. She's right. Leaving my field doesn't mean I'm giving up on scholarship. I want to be a scholar—just on my own terms. I'm no longer constrained by the boundaries of my discipline. My work is unbounded. My heart will mend. I finally feel free.

APRIL 2014

―――――

1. William Pannapacker, "On Graduate School and 'Love'," *The Chronicle of Higher Education*, October 1, 2013.
2. Ann Little, "My Bloody Valentine: Romantic Metaphors and the Academic Life," *Historiann*, February 18, 2009.
3. Syndi Dunn, "Why So Many Academics Quit and Tell," *Chronicle Vitae*, December 12, 2013.
4. Miya Tokumitsu, "In the Name of Love," *Jacobin*, January 12, 2014.

8

THE MANUSCRIPT BLUES

I can't watch *The Walking Dead*, *The Returned*, or any film by George Romero. I can't read *Warm Bodies* or reread Mira Grant's Newsflesh trilogy. There's a pile of books sitting on my office floor about zombies, including academic monographs, recent fiction, and graphic novels. I walk around them and don't glance down. Every day, a Google alert about zombies appears in my inbox, and I archive it, often without examining its contents. Zombies appear on big and small screens, in advertisements, and on social media. The cast of *The Walking Dead* and the Conehead Zombie from *Plants vs. Zombies* (the Funko Pop versions) sit on my desk. They stare at me. I try not to notice.

Zombies appear everywhere; they haunt me. I'm not afraid of the resurrected dead, but their presence makes me anxious. Why don't I just ignore them? Well, I can't. I'm a scholar who studies zombies. I should be watching television shows and movies or reading any book about the undead. I should be eagerly consuming commentaries of what zombies signify. I should be analyzing how the zombie emerges as a meme, how it's used to describe banks, politicians, and cellphone users. My research depends on doing all of these things.

I should be enthusiastic that zombies are so prevalent and popular. After all, I have an advanced book contract from an academic press to write a cultural history of zombies, which I still can't quite believe. The contract used to make me very happy. I love this project, with its combination of popular culture, ethics, and critical analysis. It is my dream project.

I'm working with a smart and forward-thinking editor who fostered this manuscript from its beginning as a mess of tentative ideas. He encouraged me to follow my instincts and transform early notions into something solid and workable. I wrote a proposal. The press liked my project and progress on the manuscript, so I got the opportunity to write a monograph on zombie media, a fun yet serious topic. (My previous research included white supremacists and doomsday prophets, so this manuscript seemed less emotionally draining.) Zombie media wasn't always easy for me to sit through—gore, violence, and all —but it finally gave me the chance to comment on a large cultural trend and think through the implications. Watching *The Walking Dead* and reading zombie fiction became work. I felt incredibly lucky.

But now I'm uneasy. My joy has been replaced by anxiety and dread.

Every time I head to my desk to work on the zombie manuscript, I turn away. I've managed to finish some shorter pieces about the undead, but I've been avoiding the bigger project. From my desk, the miniature Rick Grimes eyes me with disapproval, almost as if he knows what I'm up to. I seek something else—anything else, really—to write about. On topics like higher education, gender, and the humanities, the words come easily. I write and write and write, but not about my zombies. I've abandoned them. It's tragically funny because of how much I want to work on this project. I yearn to research and write about these monsters to figure out their cultural significance. I want to start conversations.

And yet the manuscript leaves me cold.

I'm blocked on this project, and I've never had writer's block before. It's a strange, nerve-wracking experience. My dissertation advisor once told me he didn't believe in writer's block. *One can write through anything,* he'd say. I didn't question his assertion because I hadn't encountered a problem until now. I'm stuck. I never really have been stuck for so long before. My zombie manuscript patiently waits for me to return.

I seek the causes of my writer's block. When did I stop writing the manuscript? I realize that I haven't been able to work on it since May 2013, when I quit my job. But wait. If I'm being entirely honest, that's not accurate. It was before then, in my last spring semester. I couldn't focus on the manuscript. At the time I blamed early pregnancy and changes in family life. Once I was through the first trimester, I planned to work diligently on the manuscript all summer. My family moved to Florida, which led to more upheaval. I finished a zombie eBook for a popular audience, but I couldn't find purchase on the academic manuscript. I wasn't sure I wanted to.

My academic life was on hold, so I wondered what I was

going to do. Part of me wants to fling away the manuscript along with all other academic commitments. Last spring and summer, I wanted to quit everything. I did quit a few things—an editorship and some committee memberships. Last year, rejection on the job market hit me particularly hard. I didn't want any part of the academy. I craved distance. My unfortunate zombie manuscript was just one more reminder of my failure to secure a tenure-track job. The contract, the project, is a remnant of my thwarted academic career. The manuscript is a reminder of failed dreams.

Why write an academic book if you are no longer an academic? I ask myself. *Why am I writing this book?* It won't get me a job or tenure. It won't bring me fame (which I don't want anyway). It won't pay bills. *Why am I writing this book?* I ask again and again. *Why?*

The thought of giving up on my manuscript pains me. I sob. It hurts me to think I won't finish this book. I'm no longer an academic, so why write an academic book? I can no longer write the book I was once going to.

It took me quite a while to work up the courage to email my editor. I needed to convey my despair and my hesitation about the project, and to give him an out. I composed the email, sure this was the end of my manuscript. The press could choose to abandon the project, which took my breath away.

What I realized as I typed surprised me: I can't walk away from my zombies. Instead of announcing that I'd be giving up, I wrote about my desire to make the book more of a crossover that would appeal to general audiences. I still wanted to engage people in my scholarly fascination with zombies and show them why monsters are important.

The book would still be academic in method, but not in style. As I typed, I cried about all the things the manuscript represented: dreams, disappointment, and love. I can't write for just academics anymore because I'm no longer one of them; I'm not writing to secure a job or prestige. I want to seek different conversations and broader audiences.

I want to write that book for me. The manuscript is no longer a swan song, a last hurrah for the academic career I'll never have. Instead, it is a transition remix, like everything else in my grace period. It is a link to the past, but it resides firmly in my future. This project is my refusal to be silenced, a working out of my new voice. My previous academic expectations no longer press upon me. I'm free to do the book I want to, and my editor supports me. I should have known he would; he always does.

My zombies are waiting for me, and I couldn't be happier. Miniature Rick Grimes approves.

MAY 2014

9

THINGS I MISS

I miss my commute into the university, the solace of driving in and out. The drive was my transition from home to work —thirty minutes there and back, depending on traffic. The hum of the interstate comforted me. I puzzled through research problems as I drove. I planned projects as I walked from my parking lot to my office.

I miss my office on the fifth floor of an ugly 1970s-era building. New carpet and paint balanced out by old, worn bookshelves that my department administrator had kindly rescued from surplus. I filled them with books for my courses and for current and potential projects. Texts on the Ku Klux Klan sat beside volumes on monsters. *Left Behind* graphic novels nudged *The Color of Christ*. A dog-eared cultural history of Satan ended up alongside several volumes on gender. My bookshelves presented my life as a scholar and teacher; the shelves proved intimate yet public. Students always asked about the hodgepodge as if they could know me by my books. I think they could.

Zombie posters graced the walls. The Winchester brothers of *Supernatural* resided above my standing desk, which was rigged from a short bookshelf I found in the halls. A comfy chair, another rescue from surplus, waited for students. My office was a carefully curated space that marked both who I was and who I planned to be. Pieces of my office are now scattered around my home, and some still reside in unpacked boxes. Old dreams tucked away until I'm ready.

I miss working at a university. I loved the concept of a university from the first moment I set foot on Florida State University's campus. It was supposed to be a place where ideas mattered, where thinking mattered. What it was supposed to be was never quite what it was. Yet I long for the empty buildings of summer, the hustle and bustle of the fall, and even the wearying spring.

I miss students. I always anticipated and dreaded the first day of the new semester. The copier always broke down in the middle of copying my syllabi. We sometimes had doughnuts in our office—before the department head decided they were too unhealthy, that is. Semester after semester, I still had to calm my nerves on that first day, the day when I would meet new students and reconnect with old ones. Looking around the classroom, it was a comfort to see familiar faces from previous courses, who insisted on following me from one course to the next. Their presence bolstered me. It broke my heart to tell them I was quitting.

I miss teaching. I was lucky enough to teach topics that I

found important and meaningful. I constructed syllabi for courses old and new and hoped to introduce topics familiar and strange. The classroom was my space to discuss the role of religion in our world. It was public service that I took very seriously. I wanted students to realize that religion—and religious people—were always more complicated than they first appeared. I miss making connections from course content to the larger world.

I miss the affect and habits of being at the university. My body shuffled from classroom to elevator to different buildings and into classrooms. I paced as I lectured. I walked up and down rows of students. I ran my fingers through my short hair while I processed questions and thought about my responses. Disheveled hair signaled good class discussion (or, occasionally, a class session gone awry). I punctuated lectures with animated gestures and facial expressions. One student noted on an evaluation that I was like a cartoon character. I think it was a compliment.

I miss colleagues. Lunches, hallway conversations, coffee breaks, and office chats. I miss the conversations about work, what we researched, what we taught, and what we hoped to accomplish. The lack of camaraderie is an absence yet to be filled. I miss these friends.

I miss losing myself in my work: immersing myself in books, in research, and in writing, dwelling in intellectual arguments, and scouring primary sources. The valuable time to just think is gone for now. I'll get it back soon enough, but right now, it feels like a luxury I never appreciated until it was gone.

I miss uninterrupted writing. As if on cue, the baby leans

into me and gazes into my eyes. *I'm still here*, he seems to say. I stop writing to cuddle him. Starting and stopping are my constants. I can no longer be a scholar separate from home. My life used to be scheduled, partitioned, and routine. Now, it is messier. I can't neatly divide work and home. I'm not sure I ever could anyway.

Yet the list of things I don't miss is longer: grading, department meetings, endless department emails, passive-aggressive encounters in the halls, unpaid service work, grade grubbing, the tiptoeing around faculty feuds, negotiations over class schedules, departmental hierarchies, unpaid maternity leave, and bullies. I don't miss being treated as less important than my colleagues simply because I was a lecturer. I don't miss the lack of respect. Nostalgia can't overpower the reasons I left. During my last semester, I fantasized about quitting almost every day. Some days I imagined what it would be like to pack up my office and disappear. It was clearly time for me to go.

What I miss, however, bothers me less and less as time trudges forward. My list is just a list, a record of my wistfulness. I no longer seek to dwell in what could have been. The aches and pains of transition become fainter with every passing day. I'm happier now than I have been in a long time. There are decisions to make, but not just yet. I'll be ready soon enough.

August 2014

TO WRITE OR NOT TO WRITE

What do I want to do with my life? The question makes me feel simultaneously young-ish and weary. I thought I had things figured out from point A (graduate school) to point B (tenure-track job). As you all know, I was wrong. This is the game I now play: imagining different careers and plotting the trajectories to each.

How does one go from academia to another career? What might that career be? What are the necessary steps? I'm a relentless planner, so I've developed a series of questions to help me narrow the list. Does my future career involve going back to college? No. Law school? Definitely not. Does it require a whole host of new skills? Possibly. Do I want to learn them? Kind of. Can I employ skills that I already have? Color me intrigued. Would I be happy in this new career? Maybe. This game, or the failure of my imagination, inevitably brings me back to writing.

I think I want to be a freelance writer—be paid for writing, create my own schedule, and live free of the semester system. I could be in control of my time for once. It seems liberating, exciting, and hard. One of my friends from grad school, Mike, has been urging me to take up writing for years. He first suggested it when the academic job market bottomed out in 2008. *Go be a writer*, he told me.

At the time, I was a bit offended. Was Mike hinting that I wouldn't find a tenure-track job? Abandoning my academic career for freelancing seemed like it would signal my failure as an academic. (Now that I think about it, so many things signaled my failure and so few my successes.) What I didn't realize until now was that his cajoling was encouragement. He was directing me to take an alternate career path by employing skills that I already had, and to leave the academy because I could. He was being supportive. Now, I wish I'd taken his advice sooner.

Writing is one of my favorite things about being a scholar. It came easier to me than to most academics I know. I write quickly though carefully, and I enjoy the process of researching, figuring things out, and penning what I uncover. Some days I want to bang my head against my desk. Other days are almost magical: The words flow as my analysis becomes clear and focused. Archival research became a way to not only think through historical problems but also an excuse to write.

Graduate school, then, gave me precious time to think, read, and write; I don't regret it. Scholarship was a way to develop my craft and find a voice. That was something I didn't expect as a young white woman from rural Florida pursuing a Ph.D. I found a space where my words mattered. My dissertation became a book, which still makes me proud. As academics are wont to do, I wrote for prestige and academic credibility, which is, unfortunately, code for *free* (as Sarah Kendzior points out).[1] I earned "poker chips" for a casino where I no longer gamble.[2] I've learned my lesson. Mostly.

The chance to write full time feels like the start of a new dream. But before jumping into this career, I did my research. I began by reading about writing: John Scalzi's *You're Not Fooling Anyone When You Take Your Laptop to a Coffee Shop* (2010), bell hooks' *remembered rapture: the writer at work* (1999), and Anne Lamott's *Bird by Bird: Some Instructions on Writing and Life* (2007). While Lamott and hooks engage readers in the craft of writing, hooks also lovingly describes writing as an act both radical and therapeutic. Scalzi discusses how to launch a freelance career, and his take on writing is not glamorous or romantic. Writing is simply a job, which he likes better than his other options. More important, Scalzi disdains the suffer-for-your-craft mentality (that also plagues academia) while demonstrating the effort it takes to build a viable career as a freelancer.

In addition to those books, I took two courses ($200 each) from The Thinking Writer, an online writing center created by Anne Trubek. The first course was on pitching articles and op-eds (taught by Virginia McGuire), and the second was on book reviewing (taught by Mark Athitakis). I learned about the courses on Twitter from friends and colleagues who had taken the classes. Since Trubek transitioned from associate professor at Oberlin College to freelance writer, I found The Thinking

Writer appealing because its stated goals include creating more bylines by female writers and helping academics reach larger audiences. Generally lasting two weeks, the online courses draw folks of varying skill levels, from seasoned freelancers to newbies like me. The classes offer practical, encouraging advice, especially the pitching course, and the instructors are realistic about the work required to create a financially sound freelance career. After these courses, I am less afraid to pitch possible stories, and I have had some success.

Freelance writers pitch a lot and get rejected a lot. Ultimately the successful ones piece together a variety of work for steady income from commercial copy, commentaries, and features, to name a few. This is hard work.

I'm justifiably skeptical of the romantic visions of writing, which often mimic the idyllic views of academic life. Writing could be a career for me, but it takes time and effort to build a clientele and a reputation. There are no benefits. The pay varies greatly depending on the type of writing. Articles at a variety of online news outlets and magazines pay about $100 to $250 per piece. Feature articles and print tend to pay more (if you can break into print). Some online outlets don't pay writers at all. I've written for *The Atlantic* for free. Chris somewhat frantically notes that four pieces a month equals a little less than my sad graduate stipend. I've already done the math. Because I'm home with two kids for now, I'm limited in how much work I can take on.

But, here's the thing: I am able to start a new career because of Chris's salary and benefits. I confess this privilege because I want to be honest about what an advantage this gives me over others. This is why I have a grace period. I can afford to freelance because I'm not my family's main source of income. I can build a freelance career because I don't have to worry about money. Yet.

Every time I open my laptop to write this column, I feel incredibly lucky and guilty. Chris graciously encourages and supports my career change, which means that I can temporarily afford lower pay to do what I want. That doesn't mean I should; it just means I can. I wish everyone else were so lucky.

I'm giving freelancing a chance because I want to write. Does the fact that I love it even matter? I loved academia, too, until I didn't. I did work for free because that's what an academic was supposed to do. Love convinces us to do things that harm us rather than help. Miya Tokumitsu notes the rhetoric of "do what you love" is insidious because affect replaces economic value.[3] Certain jobs become worthy of love (like academia or writing), and all the others become unlovable. My feelings about writing, then, concern me. Tokumitsu shows how academia trains us in love talk, but the reality for most academics is low-paid contingent jobs.

I refuse to be swindled again. *It's a trick, get an axe,* I tell myself. For now, I'll freelance because I like it. What do I want to do with my life? That question remains unanswered.

SEPTEMBER 2014

1. Sarah Kendzior, "Should Academics Write for Free?," *Chronicle Vitae*, October 25, 2013.
2. Caleb Crain, "Caleb Crain: How I Write," *The Daily Beast*, July 31, 2013.
3. Miya Tokumitsu, "In the Name of Love," *Jacobin*, January 12, 2014.

11

MY FIRST POST-ACADEMIC LECTURE

L ast spring, a religious studies scholar contacted me to give a public lecture at his university in September. The lecture was part of a memorial series named for one of the department's former students, Zachary Daniel Day, who died unexpectedly at age 26. His father and stepmother set up a fund to bring in scholars in the area of religion and popular culture, which was of special interest to Zach. My work on zombies fit within both categories. I had left academe more than a year and a half ago to reconsider my future, and the trip would give me an excuse to catch up with friends I hadn't seen in months who are a part of this particular department.

More important, the lecture was an opportunity to interact with scholars in my field. After I left my lecturer"s position in 2013, I was unsure whether I wanted to talk about religious studies with academics. I craved distance from the profession, but as my grace period continues, I miss those conversations. I do talk religion with folks on Twitter and Facebook, but I miss the face-to-face chats over coffee (or drinks) about religious studies, my work, and the work of other scholars. As a freelance writer now, my life is more about higher education and gender than religious studies.

The offer to speak included an honorarium and money to cover my travel expenses. A clear bonus was that the trip guaranteed three childless days, in which I could sleep without interruption, shower peacefully, and eat meals without tiny humans demanding food and/or tossing sippy cups across the room.

In many ways, the lecture seemed too good to be true. Someone wanted to pay me to talk zombies?! I could have conversations about my academic work! I could see my friends! My children's other parent was responsible for their survival! How could I not accept this offer?!

Yet, I hesitated.

I wondered if I should participate in an academic setting if I were no longer an academic. Yes, it was a public lecture to a general audience, but the previous year, a fabulous scholar on the tenure track gave it. Tucked under her name was an institutional affiliation. What label would reside under my name? Freelance Writer? Columnist? Bad Ass Ph.D.? I wondered what it would be like to look at my name absent a university affiliation. How would I feel? Joyous? Nervous? I chided myself for caring about labels. *They're arbitrary*, I told myself, *affiliation does not inherently create value.* (Does it?) Self-doubt flared. What I really wondered was: Why would this department's faculty members want me to give the lecture?

That, of course, was silly. They contacted me. They were

aware that I was no longer an academic, and they still wanted me to give the Day Lecture. "Post-academic" didn't frighten them, so why should I let labels (or lack thereof) frighten me?

I agreed to do the lecture. What I didn't realize was how happy that decision would make me.

Writing my zombie talk and creating my presentation invigorated me. I hadn't let myself think about zombies in a while, but the lecture forced me to pull together my thoughts and my analysis in ways that I hadn't before. I had zombies on the brain, and it felt good. I had to articulate why zombies matter and what cultural work they do based on my scholarly research, but in a different tone of voice. The lecture was pretty much a dress rehearsal for the tone and analysis that I want in the book I'm writing on the topic. I found that I actually wanted to work on my manuscript. Zombies are my happy place, and I guess my happy place could be worse.

I crafted and recrafted my lecture. And I did what I do best: worry. I worried about whether I was pitching the talk too high or low for my audience. I worried that Zach's family would hate it. I worried that the department, its students, and my friends would hate it. I worried that it wasn't scholarly enough. I worried that my jokes weren't funny. I worried that I no longer belonged in any setting demarcated as academic.

But something happened in the airport on my way to Tuscaloosa: I decided to stop worrying. This trip wasn't a campus visit. There was no job on the line. I didn't have to pretend to be a "serious scholar," which is a performance that I find so taxing. My goal was to have fun, and I did.

Overall, the trip was a success. My lecture went well. I

talked in some of the department's courses about blogging and online writing as well as gender and horror. With the faculty, I plotted my transition out of academia and into freelance life. I told them about how much my children dictate what I can and can't do, and how I still find myself enmeshed in my discipline in spite of my attempts to create distance. I had good conversations and meals, and more coffee than I should ever drink. For a moment, I found myself craving a tenure-track job again, but the moment passed. A stray nostalgic thought that was only a blip on the radar.

It took an academic setting to make me realize that I'm now post-academic. There will always be things that I miss, but the loss of my academic career no longer hurts as much as it once did. My path's uncharted, but it is also mine.

NOVEMBER 2014

12

HOW YOU END UP LEADING A CONTINGENCY TASK FORCE

F irst comes an email. A senior colleague in your field needs your opinion on contingent labor. You message back with your opinion. You also send links to posts, articles, and thinky pieces. Senior colleague responds, "Can we talk about contingency more?" You agree, but admit that you are no expert. Senior colleague is contacting you because you wrote a piece about your experiences as an adjunct and a full-time lecturer. You've also written about the challenges of the faculty job market and your attempt to walk away from academia. You realize that this makes you a voice on this issue. You are not sure how that makes you feel. You are writing to learn to live with how your life turned out, but you aren't sure you are an activist. People keep calling you an activist. You wonder if speaking up is the mark of activism. It makes you sad to think that's the case.

Next come the phone calls. You have a lovely chat with the senior colleague, who heads a prestigious committee for a learned society. He wants that society to take action on contingent faculty (finally). You agree wholeheartedly. This has been one of your frustrations with the learned society that you've been a part of for 12 years. Almost every year, you send money to this group for dues and conference fees. A quick calculation reveals that you've paid thousands of dollars on plane tickets and hotels to attend its annual conferences—all in an attempt to build an academic career.

You don't mention any of that in your conversation, but you could. Instead, you offer a common lament: When is this organization going to consider that scholars exist off the tenure track? What can the association do for those scholars? Senior colleague explains that the learned society is creating a task force on contingent labor. Laughing nervously, you note that it is beyond time. He agrees and asks you to stay in touch. You agree (because you are really terrible at telling people "no"). You're heartened by this development. Maybe there will be change.

Soon, emails arrive in your inbox that seem to be sussing out your interest in the task force. You are interested, so you respond. You tell your partner, who is skeptical about the whole thing. You ignore his skepticism. A conference call is scheduled with the group's executive leadership and staff. They tell you about their research into contingent-labor issues in your field. It is clear that they are in the early stages. "We need data" becomes the common refrain. You agree. Later, you worry that the emphasis on data becomes a method to delay decisions and stall the process.

During the call, you get the impression that something is brewing. Everyone is gracious and kind. The discussion is good. You start to worry about what this means for you. (You are very distrustful of people who seem nice and complimentary. You try to blame this on the cynicism about the academy, but you realize it's your survival skill for what life throws at you.) You bring your attention back to contingent faculty labor.

Someone on the call mentions that you seem to have a handle on the issue. You agree. (Agreeing seems safe.) The executive director asks you to head up the new task force. You agree without hesitation. When the executive director of your learned society asks you to do something, you do it, right? Contingent labor is a topic near and dear to you. How could you say no? What you also realize is that you have nothing politically to lose by heading the task force. You won't lose your job (because you already quit). You won't face opposition for your department because you no longer have one. Heading up the task force won't tank your job chances because you aren't applying for academic jobs. This is a safe choice for you because you've (kind of) walked away from academia.

At first, you are happy with your decision. You are chairing a task force. Your learned society cares about contingency. You will make a difference. You are very proud of yourself for taking the time to think, analyze, and push for reform about labor in academia. How noble it all seems. Bask in your nobility because it won't last long.

You insist that the committee include contingent instructors rather than just tenure-track and/or tenured professors, so you start talking to people to get them to join. You talk to a colleague who would be perfect for the task force. She asks about whether members will be paid for their service. You don't know. She mentions that service commitments exploit adjuncts as free labor, and thus, it is doubly exploitative for contingent workers on the task force. You know that she's right. This starts to bother you. You are no longer in academia. Unpaid labor has a higher cost for you than it used to. Hours spent working on the task force are hours not spent on your freelance writing. Shouldn't your work be paid for?

You realize that you still carry assumptions about service from your time as an academic. Doing service is a part of the faculty job. Without the job, you chafe at the expectation that you'll work for free. You send a politer-than-you-thought-you-could-manage email to the executive director with your concerns about exploitation and labor. You get a vacation responder. Later, you find out that the learned society is working on this question.

Time moves on.

You've been putting together the actual task force. You are supposed to be tracking the time you spend, but you sort of don't want to know. You find a slate of candidates. You suggest them. Some nominees—people who could make a difference—don't make the cut. Still, the people selected are pretty impressive and diverse, so you decide not to grumble. You've agreed to be cooperative, and you will be.

Finally, the task force is in place. A conference call is scheduled. It goes well. There's already dissension on what contingency should mean. That is utterly unsurprising. You tell task force members that we should take up the definition later. The call results in a panel at the annual meeting on contingent labor. Surprise, surprise, you agree to participate on it. (Note to self: Learn to say "no"—like right now.) There's also a reception for contingent faculty with drinks and appetizers, and task force members all get two free nights at the hotel of your choosing.

You should be excited or grateful. You are not. You feel deflated. The reception hits you the wrong way. It seems like a nice gesture. Look, the learned society is working on contingency. Have a shrimp puff! You wonder how many adjuncts could receive free registration if learned society skipped the reception. You begin to feel the burden of being in charge. Contingent labor is one of the most pressing issues for the future of higher ed. The weight of responsibility feels like too much. Your anxiety bubbles to the surface. What if you screw this up?

You hope the task force can create and accomplish goals. You want to be a part of that revolution for the learned society. You wonder if it really is a revolution.

You worry that the task force is just a dog-and-pony show. Is it possible that the task force just exists so the learned society can check contingency off its to-do list? Does the learned society want to deal with contingency in all its complexity? Or will there simply be "best practice" proposals and hand-wringing? You really hope that you are not a show pony.

You try to shake off your concerns. Playing Taylor Swift on repeat also doesn't help. You might be a show pony; you just don't know yet. You'll wait and see. All the while, you are going to insist the learned society figure out what it can do for its own members who are contingent faculty members. You also ponder why exactly you still care so much about academe. Why are you doing this labor for free? Why does this matter to you so much? You can't leave, but you can't stay either. You're stuck.

DECEMBER 2014

13

CLEAN SLATE

For at least a year and a half, I had boxes from my old university office that I refused to open. When we moved from Tennessee to Florida, and I began to pursue a career as a freelance writer, they were shuffled upstairs into Chris's office. He would occasionally grumble about their presence and move them out of the way.

I couldn't bring myself to unpack them. Besides the knickknacks and zombie kitsch, the boxes mostly held paper. So much *paper*. Reams and reams of primary and secondary sources, articles, photocopies of book chapters, Chick tracts, syllabi, lecture notes, more syllabi, green books, assignments, and student evaluations. There was also a large black file cabinet (five drawers!) full of photocopies of archival materials for my first book, notes from comprehensive exams and graduate classes, and the beginnings of various spurned projects.

As I sat down to finally open the boxes, I found my graduate training documented in hand-written notes, seminar papers, and typed exams. There was my journey from primary sources to a dissertation and from dissertation to manuscript. A ragged and torn poster from 2005 declared that I was once an "emerging scholar." The poster's condition felt like a strange symbol of early hope and promise that had been degraded by painful reality. I didn't dwell on it long as I began to look, *really look*, at the accumulated papers of my academic life. These artifacts told a story, one that I now know the ending to.

In box after box, I faced a choice: I could keep the papers safely stowed away in the attic never to be seen again or I could get rid of them.

I decided to let go.

I emptied box after box and forced the paper into perilous stacks. My academic life amounted to piles and piles and piles of white paper, a life I had abandoned resting on beige carpet. This is who I thought I would be, which is why I couldn't bring myself to get rid of it. So much of who I was was bound by what I kept in those boxes. For a long time, getting rid of the artifacts had felt too significant. Keeping all this paper became a way to assure myself I could return to academia if I wanted to.

Now I was making a different decision. I wanted to be practical. Would I really finish lingering projects on topics that I hadn't thought about in more than a year and a half? No. Did I really need the paper copies of documents that I no longer use? No. Would I really look back at my notes from graduate seminars? Definitely not. Would I return to the copies of archival documents for a book that I finished? Nope. Did I really need to keep a file of rejections from journals and jobs? No. And why did I keep such a file to begin with? (Note to all of you: Don't keep rejection files. This is where monsters lie.)

I cleared almost all of it out. I carried stack upon stack of paper down to my large green recycle bin, tossed it in, and watched it settle. Up the stairs, down the stairs, toss, watch, and move along. My recycle bin groans under the weight. I fear the amount of trees that were sacrificed for a career that didn't take. (When Chris rolled the recycling bin out to curb, the weight caused it to tip over. He chased down hundreds of pages that managed to escape and litter our street.)

There were remnants I couldn't quite bring myself to cast aside. I found a folder of notes from students. Some were quick thank-you notes and cards, but others were thoughtful letters about my teaching and courses. I also found an article about an award I won for teaching excellence at my old university. One of the committee members noted that watching me teach "restored" that person's faith in higher education, which I still think is a ridiculous sentiment to utter aloud.

The article made me pause. It brought back some of the hurt and anger that I've been working so hard to get over. I'm mostly past those raw emotions that characterized my earlier exit from academia. Granted, there are many things that still piss me off about higher education, but I tend to be content with my adjacency to academia. Yet, sitting among the detritus of my old life, I allowed myself to feel bad that I was no longer teaching. I allowed myself to be sad that nothing went according to my preferred plan, and I decided that it is truly time to move on. I'm ready. Finally.

Clearing out the boxes and the filing cabinet helped me

realize that I'm done with visions of what an academic life should or shouldn't be. Moreover, I'm done with the expectations that others still place upon me about what I should or shouldn't be doing.

I need a clean slate. I tire of what now feels like a perpetual transition. I need to move forward. Getting rid of the artifacts of a certain type of academic aspiration feels right.

I also applied for a job that would put me back in the classroom. I had very little hesitation when I decided to apply. I miss teaching. I miss students. I'm not sure what will happen, but for the first time in a very long while, I'm excited to see what does. I'm looking forward.

FEBRUARY 2015

14

MAYBE I SHOULD HAVE STAYED IN RETAIL...

W hen I was in graduate school, I worked part-time at the Gap selling jeans, t-shirts, accessories, and corporate credit cards. I had worked retail gigs on and off throughout my undergraduate years but I returned to that world in graduate school when Chris was away for the summer on an internship. I needed something to do beyond writing my dissertation. Hourly retail work fit the bill for both diversion and discounts.

What quickly became apparent was that I was different than most of the other hourly employees. They were 18 to 22; I was 26. They were single or dating; I was married. I was a manager's dream: a responsible employee. I worked my shifts without complaint, caused no drama, and covered other shifts when needed. When the summer was over, I planned to reduce my hours and focus on my dissertation and the course I would be teaching.

My manager, however, had other plans. He called me back

to his office, a tiny space adjacent to the stockroom, where he explained that the store's management team thought I was a great asset, and they didn't want to lose me in the fall. So, he offered me a promotion to assistant manager.

I was shocked by what was supposed to be good news. I offered my thanks, but I explained that I couldn't possibly take the position. I'd already promised my department I would teach in the fall, and teaching was how I earned my graduate stipend and tuition waiver.

"Don't teach then," my manager said. The store offered tuition vouchers, better pay, and a 401(k).

Startled, I glanced over at him. "Don't teach?" I repeated dumbly.

"How much is your graduate stipend, anyway?"

"$12,000 a year."

"Are you serious? That's not even minimum wage!" He grabbed the calculator off of his desk and started punching in numbers. With a flourish, he held up the calculator for me to see: My weekly take-home pay from teaching was $230.72, or roughly $5.76 an hour.

"I get an additional $2,000 for teaching in the summer," I offered weakly.

"Kelly, we'll pay you more plus benefits."

"Let me think about the offer," I managed to say as I fled the office and the store. I did think about it, but the promise of an assistant manager's job didn't seem to fit easily with graduate school. How could I turn down my stipend? Did graduate students ever turn down a stipend and work outside the university? Would my department be disappointed by my choice? What would happen to my recommendation letters? And, most worrisome: Would I struggle to finish my dissertation if I was working full-time at the Gap?

Still, a job with better pay and benefits was so tempting. I wouldn't have to pay fees for the university's health insurance. For once, I wouldn't have to take out loans to supplement my stipend and to cover the hundreds of dollars of fees that my tuition waiver didn't cover. I would make a living wage! Might this job end my constant anxiety about finances? Certainly assistant manager at the Gap wasn't my dream job, but it would pay the bills until that dream job materialized.

After days of reciting the pros and cons, I didn't take the position. I couldn't quite imagine how it would fit with my academic aspirations. Nine years later, my failure of imagination still gives me pause.

I keep thinking about that job offer from the Gap as one of the paths I didn't take. Maybe it sticks in my mind because of the years I spent on the faculty job market for a career that didn't pan out. Maybe I keep revisiting that offer because freelance writing is a constant hustle. Or maybe it is because friends are now gaining tenure. What might my life look like if I had taken that promotion and told my department to take their shitty stipend and shove it? Would I have finished my dissertation? Would I have applied for teaching jobs? Would I have been happy selling fashion jeans in all their glorious varieties? (I do love jeans.) Would I have avoided the angst, pain, and doubt of postdoctoral life?

I need an angel, preferably named Clarence (or Castiel), to guide me through the alternate endings.

The Gap, after all, is a global retailer that encompasses five brands (Gap, Banana Republic, Old Navy, Athleta, and INTERMIX) with 3,700 stores and more than 150,000 employees. Gap is the largest of the six with 1,700 stores. Assistant managers (the promotion I was offered) average salaries of $40,000 to $41,000. Gap store managers have average salaries between $63,000 and $65,000, which is five times more than my graduate-school stipend and almost three times as much as my salary as a lecturer.

The most I ever earned as a faculty member was $32,000 a year, teaching four classes for two semesters. Friends and acquaintances from my undergraduate years spent their time since then building careers. Meanwhile, I spent my 20s and early 30s in graduate school and on the job market, training for and seeking a job that is increasingly a rarity. Chris recently asked me if I knew how much money I'd lost while working in low-wage academic jobs for 11 years. I couldn't bring myself to do the math.

Turning down that promotion at the Gap seems more and more like a bad choice. I'm still paying off graduate-school loans. My mental and emotional well-being are just now recovering, almost two years after I decided to leave academe behind. Walking away from a decent-paying job with benefits was only a choice I could have made when I thought academia was my future. Now I know that future is no longer mine.

Often, I feel like I reached for too much. How could I—a working-class white woman from rural Florida—ever imagine that I could be a college professor? Did I really expect that a

Ph.D. would be my ticket into secure employment? Was it my own hubris, or naïveté, that led to such expectations?

I'm not sure. The path not taken looks better by the day because at least it was a job, not just the training for one that never materialized. Would I have had regrets if I'd become an assistant manager nine years ago? Probably, but I have them now, too. And at least I would have been paid better.

MAY 2015

15

GOODBYE TO ALL THAT

APRIL 2015

I returned my advance for *Between the Living and the Dead*. The publisher and I decided to part ways. This wasn't the press's fault.

I wasn't making progress on the manuscript. My editors wanted a full draft already. I wanted them to write a letter for a grant application to fund a year of writing; they decided they no longer wanted a cultural history of zombies. The undead, I was told, are a waning cultural fascination. The press said it would, however, take the manuscript if I could finish it quickly. For a brief moment, I thought maybe I could finish by the approaching deadline. Maybe if I put all my other writing aside....

But I couldn't really do that. Most important, I realized I didn't want to rush just to keep the contract. Instead I pulled the plug. I sent back the $1,000 the press gave me when I signed the contract in 2012. I also returned the signed document, which marked the end of my contact with the press.

I slipped into a funk about my writing, especially about writing a book that no longer had a home, and about my life more generally. I decided that I hated writing, even as I continued to write columns, personal essays, pitches, and blog posts. I wrote and wrote and wrote. Maybe I didn't hate writing; I just hated this manuscript and way it made me feel like an academic failure. I couldn't get a tenure-track job, and I couldn't finish a project I had started almost three years ago. What was wrong with me? I kept the cancelled contract in my desk as a reminder of this particular failure, but the mere thought of it left me teary-eyed. I decided to ignore both the manuscript and the returned advance.

I thought I was over beating myself up about my exit from academia. Apparently, I wasn't.

———

MAY

Out of the blue, another academic press contacted me about the manuscript. A series editor was intrigued by the project. He thought it might fit nicely with his series on American religions. I felt vaguely excited. Someone was interested in my work? My book might be resurrected? Maybe I could finish what I'd started! I had an excellent phone call with the series editor. He was enthusiastic about the book, as well as kind and gracious. He wanted to help shape it in the early stages.

The acquisitions editor for this press was similarly enthusiastic. She wanted books with a crossover potential as well as good writing and excellent research. The previous books in the series were a testament to its commitment. *Zombies are not a passing fad,* this editor said, *but an important cultural artifact.* I promised to rework my proposal and get it to her as soon as I could. I acted cheerful and positive, but I was decidedly not. I was squeamish and nervous about the manuscript. Another contract should bring me comfort, but all I felt was dread. What if I just didn't want to write this book? That question proved to be too much. There was a lurking truth that made me profoundly uncomfortable. My initial excitement disappeared. I kept stalling on the proposal. I made excuses. I worked on anything else instead.

Reaching into my desk drawer, I found my cancelled contract. I looked at my signature and shoved it hastily back in the drawer with all the other fragments of failed academic dreams.

———

JUNE

I decided to take a whole week to work only on the book proposal. I printed out both the old proposal and my newer narrative for the grant application, and headed to one of my favorite coffee shops to get some work done. With a very large and very caffeinated coffee, I started reading through the documents, which were strikingly different. The first was scholarly and jargon-laden. I talked of historiographical interventions, continuing conversations, and the books and theorists that guided my work. There were tidy chapter outlines and supposedly rousing discussions of why my manuscript mattered. I explained why American religious history needed this book and why I was the one to write it. The desperation was exceedingly clear; I wanted my discipline to need me. The second document lacked the academic tone of the first. It was more engaging. I mentioned ethics and horror, pop culture and religion, and the public humanities. I emphasized the importance of doing scholarship for larger audiences and not just for other scholars. My prose was freer and easier to read. This was the way my writing looked and read now, which made me happy. I was almost convinced that this could be a great book and that I wanted to write it. The temptation was fleeting.

I examined the two possible versions of my manuscript over and over again. I realized that I didn't really like either. Neither book spoke to me. I started crying as I packed up my things to leave. I spent rest of the week rereading my favorite books and wondering how my life had stalled in this particular way at this particular moment.

The zombie project was no longer fun for me, and truthfully, it hadn't been for a while. The only thing pushing me forward was my need to complete the manuscript simply because I had started it. But that wasn't enough of a reason to finish. Why was I trying to finish something I no longer wanted to write? The truth no longer lurked, but was visible: This manuscript was the last vestige of my academic career, the last link between who I thought I was going to be and who I am now.

I'd changed, but I hadn't really changed the manuscript to reflect that. This manuscript was never really the book that I wanted to write. It was an artifact of my frantic attempts to get a tenure-track job. I had signed the contract to make me into a more viable job candidate. I wasn't really writing it for me, but for an end goal that I couldn't reach. I finally realized that it was OK to quit the project, but it was also OK to reimagine it, too.

———

JULY

I've decided to let the project go.

"I'm not writing a zombie book," I said loudly to my empty office. "I'm not writing a zombie book," I tell Chris, my writing buddy, my middle sister, and my children, who really could not care less about whether their mom writes a book or not.

I'm strangely peaceful about my decision. There are no more tears or anguish. I even smile now as I tell people that the manuscript that could have been is not happening. I'll still write about zombies and apocalypses, but I won't write a monograph. I'm planning a series of essays on apocalypses, and I already have five essays that are begging to be written. My excitement is a bit overwhelming. I ended one project, but started another.

My new beginning is writing about endings in the ways I want to.

I'm no longer transitioning away from academic work and life. I'm moving forward, one small step at a time.

July 2015

16

WORDS TO LIVE BY

I got another tattoo. A black and gray owl with wise eyes rests on my right bicep. A locked heart lays on its chest. Its claws grasp the key. I get tattoos to mark the transitions, those shifts in my life that suggest nothing will ever be the same. Tattoos make endings and beginnings concrete. My skin changes. Inner turmoil becomes visible, and I move on.

I got another tattoo because I felt unmoored and lost. Maybe, I could force a transition with a the sting of the needles and the buzz of the tattoo gun. Maybe, I would wallow less. Maybe, there would be progress.

While I waited on the tattoo artist, Shane, to finish the sketch of my owl with locked heart, I pulled out my copy of Cheryl Strayed's *Tiny Beautiful Things*. I've taken to carrying the book around in my purse. I like the familiar heft it adds to my bag. I like to know it's always with me. These moments of indefinite waiting pass by as I reread the collection of "Dear

Sugar" advice columns that were written anonymously for The Rumpus.

What you should know is that I hate self-help books. I refuse to read them because of their overwhelming optimism about the project of the self. You have the ability to change you! Only you! And for the low price of $24.95, you might curate a nicer version of you complete with positive thoughts and success! (Fine print: All of our books ignore the structural constraints of the world, so some of you might not actually be able to curate the self you want. Sorry, not sorry.) I'm beyond skeptical about the language of self-help, as if it is so easy to change and refashion who we are.

Yet, I find myself reading and rereading a book of advice columns. I'm not even sure how I found *Tiny Beautiful Things*. I don't remember if someone recommended it or if I found the columns online. All I know is that I picked it up with deep skepticism about whether I would actually read it, and I couldn't put the book down.

When I first decided to get a new tattoo, I planned to get some of Strayed's phrases tattooed on my wrists:

"Let yourself be gutted."

"Art isn't anecdote."

"Be brave enough to break your own heart."

"Every last one of us can do better than give up."

I couldn't quite decide which of the phrases, which I murmur to myself throughout the day, should become permanent. There were too many possibilities. Dear Sugar's advice would have scrawled from my wrists up my forearms. Her words would bump up against the tattoos I already have.

Wrists and forearms would not be enough. Shoulders, calves, thighs, and back would also have to bear Sugar's wisdom. From shoulders to feet, I would be covered in words, her words.

I chose the owl, a symbol of wisdom and learning, instead.

What I realized as I reread *Tiny Beautiful Things* in that tattoo parlor is that I already carry Strayed's words with me. Her words have become my words. I've applied what she writes to own life. I don't need them etched on my flesh because her words help me live. Her advice, given to other people, saves me from myself. This is more than any other book has done.

On the tough days, when fatigue settles on me like a heavy coat, and disappointment leaves a bitter taste in my mouth, I long for someone to call me "sweet pea." For someone to urge me to move forward. I manage to get stuck in my own suffering. I tend to wallow. And yet, Sugar tells me to reach, so I do. I grumble about how hard it is to reach, but I reach anyway. Sugar reminds me: "Nobody will protect you from your own suffering." No one will, Kelly, no one. My mantra becomes: "Every last one of us can do better than give up." Do you hear me, sweet pea, don't give up. I hear you, Sugar, and I'm listening.

My best friend and I have taken to calling Strayed Saint Cheryl. We recite the words of *Tiny Beautiful Things* as if they are litany, or maybe even a prayer. We text her wisdom back and forth. Dear Sugar emerges as my newfound moral compass. She's empathetic, humane, compassionate, and unrepentant. She's everything I've sought in a religious institution, and what I've never found. If she could see me, I bet she wouldn't turn away.

My owl tattoo has healed nicely. I've reread the book once more to find the wisdom that I might have missed. The pages have started to show wear. There are underlines in different colors, notes and scribbles. I rewrite her advice in the margins to teach my mind and body which of her words matter most.

The advice that I write over and over is: "The fuck is your life. Answer it." It is Sugar's response to that incredulous question: WTF?! That question we so often employ when we can't comprehend what's happening to us. I repeat Strayed's answer aloud in my office and disturb the two sleeping dogs. It is the hardest advice for me to handle. Suffering happens to us. Life happens to us. Sometimes, we can't comprehend either, but they are ours. They make us who we are. We can't shy away from that truth; we have to own it.

Strayed's columns have encouraged me to see myself. To face those beautiful and awful truths of who I am with compassion and love. To reckon with the fuck that makes up my life with grace. She encourages me, and all the other readers, to "tackle the motherfucking shit out of love." In *Tiny Beautiful Things*, I find love, acceptance, truth, intimacy, openness, gratitude, and an appreciation of life's messiness. There's no stark certainty here. No punishing judgment. Just a vision of how fucked-up life can be and the importance of radical empathy.

Saint Cheryl, full of grace, thank you for your advice.

AUGUST 2015

17

35

In August, I turned 35. I expected an existential crisis, or, at least, a temporary breakdown. This is how I've spent previous birthdays since about 25. I'm ambivalent about birthdays. I want them to bring me joy. I want to have fun. But, instead, I end up accounting what I accomplished each year and whether those accomplishments actually added anything to my grand plan of "how my life should go." I confronted my failures. I vowed to do better the next year. And I updated my list of what I need to accomplish by the next year.

My birthday would come and go. Some years, I would be pleasantly surprised at what I was able to do. My checklist was coming along nicely. My life had purpose and drive. I would be successful. Other years, disappointment left a bitter taste in my mouth. I was a failure. My career was not turning out as I planned. I would work harder. I would sleep less.

Looking back, I do realize that this was a not-very-nice thing to do to myself. I still can't quite believe that I would fall into the same stupid trap year after year.

August 15 became a day of reckoning rather than a day of celebration. This year, I steeled myself for the onslaught. The week before my birthday I prepared myself for the crisis that I knew was coming. The days dragged by, but I felt fine. I looked at calendar again waiting for the angst to hit me hard, to stop my breath, and to make me want to hide until the damn day was over. My life was no longer anywhere near the grand plan. Where was my crisis?

August 15 came and went. I felt fine. What in the heck was happening? I started to freak out because I fumbled my annual breakdown. This was a yearly ritual. This was an attempt at self-reflection, a brutal one, but still an attempt. I waited for the panic to wash over me. There was no panic. I tried to dredge up a tiny bit of anxiety. Anxiety never materialized. I pulled out the big guns: One day I was going to die. Still nothing. What would happen to me if I didn't do the accounting? Nothing at all. I held onto this insight tightly before it dissipated. I wanted to etch it onto my brain. To make it permanent. *Nothing at all*, I repeated aloud. NOTHING. AT. ALL.

The melodramatic focus on accomplishments was not ever about my life, but the career that I thought I wanted. It was a to-do list that a younger version of me created. My plan equated life with career and career with success. A career is not a life. What an impoverished vision of success dependent on external validation and a weird obsession with success as our only option. Accomplishments are an awful way to measure the value of a life.

Sometime between 34 and 35, I decided that building a career was less important than building a life. There are more humane ways to live. I've learned more from my supposed failures than I ever have my successes. Failures made me rethink, reimagine, redo, or reorient. When I failed to achieve the life I thought I was supposed to have, I started to realize my imaginings of life were the start of my problems. I was never failure, but I was measuring the wrong things. When life moved, I finally moved with it. I was better than fine. My birthday became a day that showed I made it through another year. For once, that was enough. It always should have been.

AUGUST 2015

18

A CONVENIENT STORY

I'm confronting a strange sense of déjà vu. Recently, I've alternated between studying for the GRE, writing a personal statement, wrangling both kids by myself (Chris is on travel for work), and relying on coffee to keep me mostly alert.

I feel that I have done this process of applying for graduate school before because I have. In 2001, I applied for my M.A. in Religion. Now 14 years later, I'm applying yet again, but this time for an M.F.A. in Creative Writing with a focus on creative nonfiction. The process feels simultaneously familiar and strange. I know what's expected of my application. I can prepare. I can still get hives from worrying about a test. Yet, I never expected to consider graduate training again in the middle of my 30s. I imagined a different life than the one I have.

My life changed significantly in 14 years. I'm married with two children. Our 14th anniversary is in December. The cat remains mean, but she's less playful. The first dog is older, grayer, and deaf. There's a younger dog, but she's already middle-aged by canine standards. My sister got married, so did my brother. I now have a niece and nephews. My grandmother died. I haven't spoken to my biological father since 2007. I earned a Ph.D. and never found that career I trained for. I started freelance writing.

At 35, I find myself wondering less about what happened to deliver me to this particular point and more about what comes next. What are the possibilities? What are my constraints? The last time I wrote a personal statement I was 21. I was earnest, naïve, confident, and ambitious. Life would go according to my plans even if I had to force things to happen the way I wanted them to. I was in control. (I needed the illusion of control.) The world would obviously cater to my whims if I worked hard and did what I was supposed to.

I still encounter glimmers of that younger version of me. I feel her need for certainty and assurance. I still give into her desire for control and order, especially in the chaos of a seven-year-old and a two-year-old. Her deep yearning to belong somewhere still resides in my bones, but feels less urgent and demanding. I'm no longer her. Until I started writing my personal statement for my M.F.A. application, I didn't realize how far gone she was.

This new statement about me reads differently from the previous version. I had to find the words to explain where I had been to signal where I wanted to be. The present must reckon with the past and the future. *Where had I been?* was a deceptively easy question. I knew this story. I've been telling some version of it for two years. It is rote and comforting. I went to grad school, got a Ph.D., found only contingent jobs, took a couple years off, "quit" academia, and now freelance write. Nothing new to see here. Move along. You've heard it all before.

What I realized is that this story of who I am is too convenient. It misses all my starts, stops, flailing, and attempts to change direction. It ignores that I couldn't cleave off my academic identity even when I tried to and that I still hoped for the future I worked toward for years. It misses the mourning, grief, and anguish with an easy resolution (new career!).

The timing was also off. This story began at the wrong place. It started too late. I should have pushed back further to that anxious girl from Jackson County, Florida, who was never sure of her place in the world. How she clung so tightly to a version of success that would take her away from home. How she loved home and hated it for as long as she could remember. How far, far away seemed so appealing and safe. How she desperately hoped getting away would make life easier. How tired she was of hard and complicated and divorce. How she learned to run away. How the distance would come to break her heart.

This story also tried to end before the end. The girl was no longer a girl. She was a woman, a partner, and a mother. Running away couldn't save her from suffering, and she did suffer because we all suffer. She finally realized that she had always been a writer, but this wasn't the end. This was not redemption. This was not the page turn she hoped for. She writes to pay for daycare and other bills. She writes to have something to do. She writes to fight off boredom and melancholy. She writes because there are things she still needs to say. She writes as a way to live in this world. She writes to find meaning. She writes to face her suffering because running away never really helped. She writes because there are moments where she still feels lonely and lost and unmoored. Lately, she writes to understand where she came from and who she would like to be. She writes to express what she can't make herself say aloud. She writes to live.

This story I've told myself is no longer enough. It doesn't reach. It doesn't say where I want to go. It is too tidy. Too neat. Too emotionally removed. Partially, that's because I've been unsure of what I wanted to do next. I had been avoiding the future and trudging cautiously through the present. I feared new dreams because previous ones only led to disappointment. Not dreaming is a safe and terrible way to live. The fear of failure kept me from imagining what is possible. I'm done with those fears. If I fail, at least I'll know I've done something.

I'm applying for an M.F.A. because it is nice to dream again: to imagine what might come next and dwell in the possibilities.

Years ago, I wouldn't have imagined my life as it stands now. My options were narrow and strict. And now, I'm grateful for all of the possibilities. I'm surprised by the narrowness of my vision. Life shifted and offered up different possibilities that I wouldn't have ever considered. I had fall off my desired path to be able to see the other paths available to me.

I had to get lost to be found.

Writing my personal statement brought me clarity that I've been seeking for months. My story isn't working for me anymore, so I need to work toward a new one.

Yesterday, my toddler found the Post-It notes that I used to brainstorm my personal statement and put them all over his belly. He was so proud of his "stickers," as he showed them to me. His sister and I giggled at his choice of body art, and I couldn't help but think this is my life right now. My story's unfolding, and I can't wait to see what happens next.

NOVEMBER 2015

19

ONE MORE SET OF RECOMMENDATIONS

L ast fall, I received an email from a former student asking for recommendation letters—assuming that I remembered him. I did. He took two of my courses while I taught at my previous university. His email was surprising because I get such requests for recommendations less frequently now.

I quit teaching after the spring semester of 2013, so many, if not most, of my former students have moved on. They've had other lecturers or professors recommend them for graduate, medical, or law school or whatever other opportunities they were pursuing. Until I received this email, I imagined that I had written all of the recommendation letters that I was ever going to write. Teaching was a faint and fading memory.

This particular student, however, hadn't forgotten about me, and I hadn't forgotten about him. He was creative, smart, and reserved but eager to discuss the course readings. His papers were some of my favorite to read. He wrote about what horror movies teach us about American culture and how zombies represent us back to ourselves. When he emailed asking for recommendation letters for M.F.A. programs in screenwriting and film, I wasn't entirely surprised. He would be fantastic at either, and any program would be lucky to have him.

Yet, I couldn't help but laugh when the email arrived, and maybe groan a little bit, too. Over dinner, I told Chris, "I just got asked to write recommendation letters to M.F.A. programs." He grinned. I mockingly glared at him. The irony was a bit too much for both of us because I'd been planning to apply to an M.F.A. program myself—in creative nonfiction.

In short, I would be both the recommender and the recommended. That turn of events left me unsettled. For a moment, I felt simultaneously ancient and young. After all, my student was at the beginning of a potential career, and I am still trying to figure out what I want to be when I grow up.

Moreover, I tried to tell myself that applying to M.F.A. programs at this point in my life was a lark, but I knew it wasn't.

Months earlier, I had participated in a workshop on storytelling as a way to figure out if writing was the career I wanted to pursue. When one of my fellow participants found out where I lived, she encouraged me to apply to the local university's M.F.A. program in creative writing. She had been accepted by the program and loved the faculty, but had instead chosen to attend a university closer to home. "You would love an M.F.A.," she enthused, but I wasn't so sure. I had already completed grad school once. I had a Ph.D., yet that journey hadn't ended quite where I had hoped it would. Did I want to go back to school? Was I willing to apply and commit to another graduate program?

I tried to table the idea, but it took hold in my mind. Spending two to three years working on the craft of my writing was appealing. I did want to nerd out on sentences. I researched the local M.F.A. program, chatted up former faculty, and met with one of its professors. After buying my coffee, he asked if I was applying to the program with the hope of securing a gig teaching writing. "No," I said cheerfully, "I tried that before, and it didn't work out." I explained that I wanted the time and space to become a better writer and the support of a writing cohort to work on manuscripts that I already envisioned. At the end of our conversation, he encouraged me to apply.

So I did—even as I lowered my expectations. I told myself firmly that I just needed to see what would happen and that I wouldn't count on this application in a way that would invite heartbreak. I would be aloof and chill.

My last round of applying to graduate school was in 2001, so I had forgotten what a hassle it is. But something happened as I filled out the paperwork. I became not just excited but invested in my M.F.A. application. This felt like the next step in my path, so I allowed myself to be both determined and hopeful. I studied and retook the GRE. I requested transcripts. I wrote and rewrote a personal statement. I redrafted an essay as my writing sample.

All the while, I wrote and rewrote my former student's recommendation. My familiarity with the application process helped me write a better recommendation letter because I knew how much this mattered to him and what one letter might mean for his future.

At the same time, I delayed emailing my own recommenders. Reaching out to them again made me feel vulnerable and weary: This would be yet another request for yet another letter. I was inviting their judgment, their opinions, and possibly their disdain. For a terrible moment, I felt like an academic failure. I judged myself by academic standards of success and didn't like what I found. The moment passed quickly; they tend to these days. I took a deep breath and acknowledged that I had already moved on.

Still, I emailed my recommenders with trepidation. My previous requests were always about potential jobs and my academic work. The life I left behind was the one they had trained me for. This request felt fraught and tense. I was asking them to look beyond the path I decided not to follow and imagine another path instead. I was asking them to do what I had been doing for almost two years.

My worries were misplaced. Each of my recommenders reacted with enthusiasm and pride, just like I had with my own student. One, who is now a dear friend, noted that this might be where I was supposed to be all along.

I wrote my letter for my student; they wrote mine.

My student sent off his applications in November, and I uploaded his recommendation letter with a grin and happy thoughts. I sent off my own application in early December. We're both eagerly waiting to hear whether we got into our respective programs.

My student emailed after I sent off all of his letters. He

thanked me for recommending him. But, he also said more. My courses, he explained, helped him become "a more engaged and analytical thinker." I saved his email in a file with similarly kind notes I've received from other students. That file is the archive of the life I left behind—a life I often still want, but not as much as I used to. There are other files that remind me of the life I'm reaching toward now and all of its potential.

JANUARY 2016

20

WITHOUT MEANING TO

I search for meaning everywhere. In television shows, theme songs, top-40 hits, novels, Internet memes, and casual comments from friends and strangers. I look for meaning in relationships. In the words, spoken and not. In the emotions that radiate in gestures, silence, frowns, smiles, and tears. I look for meaning in the people that surround me. There are the small hands that reach out to hold mine. There are kisses and hugs. There are fleeting touches and glances that shift away. There's the intimacy of sharing a life for years and knowing what this body communicates. I search relentlessly for the meaning of a life, my life, theirs, or maybe even yours.

Truth appears and recedes, but meaning feels just out of my grasp. I'm searching for something, but I'm never sure what. At moments, I feel I'm on the cusp of discovery. But then, the search tugs and pulls me in a different direction. Discovery becomes a dead end. Meaning seems almost tangible, and I reach out for it frantically. I can never be certain it is directed at me.

The television blares in my living room. The theme song from one of my daughter's favorite television shows catches my attention. My daughter, her best friend, and my son dance wildly to its catchy beat. The song urges me to be who I wanna be "yeah, yeah." The children sing along loudly and enthusiastically. The girls know the words; my toddler sings the words he thinks he hears. Their joy is infectious. I stop to watch them dance and sing. They don't have the time for existential questions meaning or identity or belonging in the world. Their lack of concern makes me a bit envious.

As I enter and exit my car, a particular song plays on the radio. It's an anthem that still manages to be mopey. The singer assures me that "one match can make an explosion." Its heavy repetition on the radio captures the attention of both of my children. My toddler falls in love with this song. He marches around the house singing "This is my FIGHT song" at the top of his lungs. Occasionally, he punctuates his singing with chops and kicks. He missed the song's meaning and made up his own.

For months and months, this song remains stuck in my head, and it followed me into the new year. I find myself humming it as I pour cereal into bowls each morning, when I wash dishes, pick up toys, as I go to my desk to write, or when I move around my house to and from my office. Sometimes, humming isn't enough, and I sing "I have a lot of fight left in me." This lyric reassures me. I do have fight left. But, singing along is also my attempt to rally. To reach down deep and find that fight, especially when I don't want to. There are days that I'm not sure what I'm fighting. Is it boredom, anxiety, stress, or worry? Am I fighting for my space in the world? Am I learning to inhabit that space? Or is my fight really a search for meaning that I can't quite find?

The song doesn't always reassure. It claws at me too. Scratches and wounds. I sing quietly: "all those things I didn't say are wrecking balls inside my brain..." Words do bang around in my brain. Constantly. That's the writer's burden. I wonder if I can just get them down on the page, maybe the words will leave me alone.

I keep looking for what all of this means. I'm not sure what I've found.

The meaning I find is mostly reassuring. Messages about being the person you are or becoming the person you want to be. Authenticity, or maybe realness, emerges as the desired goal. If only you can be who you are, everything else will follow. These are easy messages that point to a vague truth that feels almost right. Or at least, something close enough to truth to fool us.

Be yourself, yeah, yeah, because that's what you are supposed to do. Slip off one self, put another on. Carry on.

I bristle at the suggestions. I try to imagine how one would know what is authentic. How do you claim the real? How do you know what you've found? But, more importantly, what might it all mean?

This is where I flail away from messages that seem too easy. This is where I get stuck, and I start to search again. I've chased meaning or transcendence or truth throughout my life, and nothing manages to stick. The habits never take. The popular wisdom leaves me cold. I start to search again.

This is when I begin to wonder if maybe meaning isn't what I hope it will be. Maybe the meaning I seek won't offer explanations, soothe hurts, or make the world more intelligible. Maybe the search is what matters. Maybe pursuing meaning is the best that I can hope for. Maybe I'm seeking something big when I should focus on something smaller, like a chubby toddler hand in mine. Maybe I found the meaning I seek was always there, I just didn't know what to look for.

JANUARY 2016

MISSED TURN

I woke up on Sunday convinced that I had no words left. That I had nothing to say, and perhaps, I was done as a writer. That I had already written my best essays. That I had no good sentences left in me. I was out of words, phrases, sentences, paragraphs, and pages. I was done.

Sundays are rarely writing days for me. Weekends are family time, so I let my partner and kids distract me from the angst chasing me. They are always my favorite distractions.

On Monday morning, my alarm on my watch buzzed me at 4:45 a.m. There was a plane to catch to Harrisburg, Pennsylvania. I had been invited to Elizabethtown College, where my friend, Richard, teaches, to give a reading at Bowers Writers House. My reading was from an essay on Dozier School and my hometown, one of the most personal essays I've ever written. (A story that is still unfolding and that I am chasing as hard as I can.) The day before I was to be a visiting writer, I was convinced that I might no longer be able to write. The irony was not lost on me. My angst was fitting, and truth be told, somewhat expected. My writing life can be narrated as story of doubt, angst, and anxiety. I keep trying to tell another story, but this is the narrative that continues to emerge.

As I pulled out of my driveway, I probed this fresh (and melodramatic) concern about writing. Out of the neighborhood, take a left, pass construction and new development, take a right, drive past big churches and small churches, other neighborhoods, stop at red lights, and take a right onto Interstate 10 to get the airport. The interstate snaked in front of me, but the darkness of the early morning meant I could only see what the headlights made visible.

Why, I thought, *did I feel like I had nothing left to say?* Was I not nourishing my creativity? Were there no more stories for me to tell? Was I actually running out of words? This seemed improbable, impossible even. Of course, there are still things I want to write. At any given moment, there's a revolving set of essays stored in my head, on to-do lists and Post-it notes, and in my journals and planner. Perhaps, what I really meant was that there are topics on which I have nothing left to say. Topics that no longer interest me. This could account for some of my fatalism, but not for all of it.

While trying to figure out my anxiety about writing, I noticed the sign for mile marker 190 on the interstate. I missed my exit to the airport six miles ago. On I-10 outside Tallahassee, the next exit was nine miles away. I looked at the darkened road stretched before me and slammed one hand on the steering wheel. I could cut across the median, but it is uneven with sharp inclines and declines. The morning was too dark to navigate it safely. I didn't want to wreck my car in a stupid attempt to make my plane.

"FUCK," I screamed. And then, I screamed in frustration. And screamed again. With my rage expressed in a mostly wordless howl, I began to breathe deeply. I briefly comprehended why my toddler yells in anger. The sense of calm that settles on you afterward feels pretty spectacular.

I kept driving. Miles passed by quicker than I imagined: one, two, three, four, and then nine. I turned onto exit 181 and managed to get back on interstate headed in the right direction. I would make it to the airport in time for my flight, but I could feel the tension taking over my shoulders. I needed to make it there soon. "Typical," I muttered, "This is typical. I get distracted and miss a turn."

But, I only missed a turn. I was able to make it again when I had another chance. I made my flight and then the next. When the plane touched down at Harrisburg International Airport, there was snow piled on the edges of the runway. It was grey and slushy and beautiful. I snapped a picture of the snow for my daughter.

When I gathered my purse and laptop to deplane, I found myself thinking again, *What if I have nothing left to say?* Hell of a visiting writer I was going to be. Visions of cherubic undergrads asking me about the writing life bounced around in my head. Wide eyes and eager smiles waiting patiently for me to disperse wisdom. What would I even say? I got a handle on my nerves as I walked through the concourse, by security, and beyond baggage claim. By the time I reached the parking lot, I decided to table all of my concerns and enjoy my time with Richard and his students. Angst can always wait.

Hours later in my warm hotel room, Chris called to check in. We talked about a recent post by John Scalzi on Impostor Syndrome.[1] He sent it to me earlier, and I read and tweeted about it. I admitted that I live and breathe doubt as a writer. This was likely nothing new to Chris. We've been married 14 years. He knows me and my neuroses pretty well. But still, the moment felt like a confession.

"I look over my essays and wonder what if I've written the best essay I'm ever going to write? Or the best sentence?"

I can almost feel Chris's smile through the phone. I close my eyes and imagine his dimples and the mischievous glint in his eyes. He laughs his easy laugh, one of things that I love most about him.

Teasingly, he asks, "That sentence from the last issue of *Women in Higher Education*? Or maybe the best word is from your 'I look like a professor' essay?"

There's a dramatic pause. "What if your best word is 'the'?"

I dissolve into giggles. "I'm pretty sure my best word is 'asshole' in the upcoming issue."

We laugh together.

After the call ends, I recognize that this is my familiar anxiety before a break through. That I'm not so much afraid that I have no words left, but that the words that I have to give are part of a bigger project, likely a book. That I'm finally ready to direct my creative energies to something else. I have newer and different things to say.

I'm at a beginning, and I'm terribly afraid. The road is dark.

The headlights only illuminate a few feet in front of me. I'm not sure I'll make my exit, but I'll get another chance. I keep driving anyway.

FEBRUARY 2016

———

1. John Scalzi, "Impostor Syndrome, or Not," *Whatever*, January 30, 2016.

WRITING ADVICE

I detest giving advice. No, that's not a strong enough sentiment. I *hate* giving advice, so I generally avoid giving it unless someone forces my hand. Advice pretends to be universal, though it really isn't. Our situations are particular, complex, and fraught, and advice rarely brushes the surface of this complexity. Advice pretends to be applicable to everyone while knowing it never is. I'm leery of people who willingly offer up advice, especially unsolicited advice. *I didn't ask*, I want to say, but never do. I often wonder what those who spout advice envision human experiences to be, and I figure what they envision looks remarkably similar to their lives. Something worked for them, so it must work for us? Their certainty makes me twitchy. I usually look for an exit.

It is hard for us to imagine the lives of others, their circumstances, their situations, and their constraints because often we aren't aware of our own. How do we get outside our own heads long enough to grapple with someone else's reality?

(Can we?) This is why I hate giving advice because of the needed particularity. I understand fully that life is hard, but what if I can't imagine the particularity of that hard for you? I know there are others who can't quite imagine why a task takes Herculean effort from me and barely any from them. What advice can I offer you without knowing more about your situation? Some of the most common advice that I've received proved to not work for me, and I beat myself up about it for a while. I tend not to now. Advice is cheap; lots of people clamor to offer it up. When someone asks me for advice, I hesitate and pause and usually fumble the question. This is also why I tend to be brutally honest about my own situation. I provide the context for what I end up saying, even then, I still hate giving advice.

Three weeks ago, I did a reading in front of audience of mostly undergraduates. This was my first reading, and I wasn't entirely sure what to expect. I made it through the last paragraph of my essay and choked up. This essay is one of the personal and vulnerable that I've every written. I read and reread it aloud because some of the paragraphs were hard for me to get through without tears. I made it through, but the last few lines hit hard. I took a gulp of bottled water and another, cleared my throat, and waited for questions. The undergrads were hesitant, but they started asking questions, good ones about craft, research, process, and audience. The last question of the evening came from my friend, Richard, who asked what kind of advice I would have liked to hear as an undergraduate about being a writer. The question, one I should have seen coming, threw me.

I paused to gather my thoughts and then offered up the first thing that came to mind: "I never imagined I could be a writer."

What I realized as I rambled through my answer was that no one even suggested I could be a writer while I was an undergraduate. At the community college I attended, before I headed off to the university, professors assured me that I would make a good teacher, not professor, or nurse, not a doctor. I worked for the campus newspaper and later became the editor, but no one thought to mention that I could be a writer. Maybe, they assumed I would figure it. Maybe, they didn't. This was rural, northern Florida. Writing didn't seem like a practical career choice. When the newspaper hosted a writer from a nearby town, he was a forty-something white man who thought he was funnier and smarter than he actually was. I left his talk wondering if all writers were assholes. He was not an example I wanted to emulate. Professors explained that my writing was good, but I had a keen sense it was somehow not good enough. (One professor, however, encouraged me to write more and keep writing. I'm forever grateful to him.)

I was smart, but the creative life didn't appear as an option. No one was encouraging a working-class white girl from a trailer park to pursue writing as a dream or a career. That opportunity seemed to closed to me, so why waste time pursuing it? And I didn't. I took the long way back to writing.

All of this came out of me in a rush of words. The undergrads looked at me, and I looked back at them. They blinked. I did too.

I hadn't given them a real answer to the question. Instead, I was making my way to an answer. I smiled brightly and apologized for rambling. "What I meant to say is I needed to hear, more than anything else, that my voice was enough." Wanting to write was enough to be a writer. At 18, 19, or 20, I wished someone took the time to tell me that my perspective was unique. That the only person who could write like me was *me*. That I shouldn't try to be someone I wasn't. That my background, the places where I landed, made me who I was. That this place that birthed me might not be New York City or San Francisco or Boston and that was okay. That this place, that no one had ever heard of, created me and pushed me to be a writer. That I shouldn't try to be someone I wasn't. That I could emulate other people's writing styles on the way to finding my own. That there was something about my voice that needed to be heard. That writing would give me the chance to speak and be heard. That my voice mattered. That my writing mattered to me and that was enough.

I wish someone had told me to trust myself and my writing, so I wanted them to trust themselves and write how, when, and what they want. Also, I explained that you can't run from who you are or where you are from. I tried running away more than once. And yet, I was standing in front of them reading an essay about my hometown. I moved away (ran away) 15 years ago, but here I was reckoning with my roots in public. How unseemly and delightful and indicative of what I write. Running away never quite works the way we hope it would. I was standing before them as evidence of this fact.

Own your story and the places that made you. And write what feels the most authentic to you. These undergrads might have gotten more than they bargained for, but I wanted them to hear someone say that what they write matters. And that they matter as writers.

Here's what else I wish I had said to them: Write because you want to write. Just wanting to is *enough*. Write because what you write matters. Remember that always, especially because there are plenty of jerks in this world who will tell you otherwise. Write because you want to speak. Write because you want to be heard. Write because anyone can be a writer.

You just have to write and keep writing.

P.S. Don't let anyone tell you how to write either. Writers write when they can. Figure out what works for you. And you don't have to write every day (Daniel José Older[1] beautifully explains why this is nonsense, and so does Sarah Boon[2]).

FEBRUARY 2016

———

1. Daniel José Older, "Writing Begins With Forgiveness: Why One of the Most Common Pieces of Writing Advice is Wrong," *Seven Scribes*, September 9, 2015.
2. Sarah Boon, "Writing By Your Own Rules," *Creative Nonfiction Collective Society*, September 24, 2015.

23

LOSING OUR SELVES, BUT NEVER
GETTING LOST

There's a book both of my kids love for me to read to them, *The Monster Who Lost His Mean* (2012). The Monster loses his custom M, which is where his Mean comes from. Now, he's just the Onster. Instantly, he becomes a social pariah. None of the other Monsters will eat with him at lunch. *Boom boom! Crunch crunch! The Onster sits alone for lunch.* They tease and abandon him. *Boo hoo! Sigh sigh. The Onster's sad and starts to cry.* There's only so much unkindness the Onster can take, so he leaves the Monster Wood. The book traces his frantic search for his Mean and his journey to finding a new and different place in the world. It is a book about transitions, identity, and feelings. I love the Onster more than they do, which is probably why they request that I read this book over and over again.

"Wead it again," my toddler demands, and I do.

When my daughter was in pre-Kindergarten, she selected, *The Monster Who Lost His Mean* from the Scholastic catalog. She and I would open it up to see what new books we could find, and we would circle in crayon the books we hoped to purchase. Like me, she loves books. She also knows that I have an enduring fascination with monsters, so I think that's what drew her to this particular book.

We first read about the Onster in those early days of her brother's life. When he was an infant, he would sleep as we read. I had two children instead of one, and I was grimly determined that my daughter not feel displaced by her brother. I would arrange her brother to rest on top of my chest and read books to her. Any book she wanted. I would nurse and read. And read and read and read. She would sit as close as she possibly could and her hand would gently touch her brother as if she were checking to make sure he was real. Both children snuggled close as I read a story about a Monster whose life was turned upside down.

The Onster was one type of creature, and then, he wasn't. He was suddenly something else. What in the world was he supposed to do? He tried valiantly to reclaim that previous identity. If only he could find his Mean, then everything would return to normal. If only he could go back. His Mean remains missing. But, the Onster learns to be someone else. Someone kinder and more considerate. The thing that he lost was worth so much less than what he finds: friends, kindness, and community.

Yet, the Monsters aren't impressed by his transition. (Mean people often aren't.) They refuse to leave him alone, so the Onster decides to try and be mean. He fails spectacularly. He can't bring himself to be mean just because those awful Monsters think he should be.

Disappointment slouches his shoulders. His head hangs low. The Onster is dejected. When he is at his lowest, his new friends (human children, of course) throw him a surprise party complete with cake and balloons. The last line of the book is "He's happier in every way."

The first time I read this book I was only a few months into my decision to take a break from academia. I was sleep deprived because my son woke me up every two hours to nurse. I was tired and spent. I read *The Monster Who Lost His Mean* to my daughter and felt like maybe the book was as much for me as it was her. The Onster survived transitions, and so could I. He not only survived, but thrived. Just because he lost something didn't mean he was lost. Losing his Mean provided the Onster with a different set of opportunities that he couldn't have imagined before.

Anytime my oldest gave me a choice in what we read, I picked up this book. Reading it aloud to her gave me the excuse to read it again for myself. There were days when we read it multiple times. *Boom boom! Crunch Crunch! Boo hoo! Sigh sigh.* I always paused when he started to cry. When sleep deprivation and my own transitions became too much, I would shed a few tears with him. Even struggling fictional characters need solidarity.

The Onster lost his Monsters. I lost my place in academia (or gave it up, really). Neither of us lost ourselves.

As my daughter found other books that she liked better, we stopped reading *The Monster Who Lost His Mean* with our previous intensity. Instead, we picked up Olivia, Skippyjon

Jones, Fancy Nancy, and Dr. Seuss. Then, we stopped reading it altogether.

Over a week ago, my son, now two years old, found this book crammed between other books on the shelves. "Wead it," he said. He and I read it together while his sister reads a book on her own. She doesn't need me to read aloud to her anymore, but she still likes me too. It feels like I've lost something important, but I gained something too. I tear up a bit when we get to the last line.

"Mama, wead it again," he declares. And I do, all the way to the end. The Onster is still happier in every way, and I am too.

Neither of us was ever truly lost. We just had to find another way.

FEBRUARY 2016

24

HOW YOU END UP LEAVING THE
CONTINGENCY TASK FORCE

Yery ou leave not with a grand exit—a clear resolution to the problem of contingent labor in religious studies—but with repeated sighs of frustration (and private rants to your beleaguered partner). Your exit from the task force you were asked to lead in your disciplinary society is a gradual one. It is a slow goodbye. (You hate slow goodbyes.) You realize that you started to imagine your exit strategy not long after your entrance. That is never a good sign.

You remember the moments that led to your departure with a painful clarity—like the time you attended a workshop on contingent labor directed toward department chairs. You put on your nice clothes, dress pants, blouse, and navy blue cardigan, and your glasses because you wanted to be taken seriously. You put on your game face. You were ready to talk about contingent labor in higher ed. You made awkward conversations at lunch with a smile and a nod. It all took a turn when a department chair suggested that adjuncts liked, no, loved their jobs in spite of low pay and prestige. In that moment, you took a deep breath and tried not to scream.

There's also the difficulty you faced convincing full professors that yes, you were actually the chair of the task force —not the co-chair or someone's assistant. Yes, someone who looks like you could be in charge and knowledgeable about the topic.

The moment you decided you were done was in a panel discussion on the modern university and contingency last November. When a full professor suggested that tenured and tenure-track academics were powerless to do anything to help contingent faculty, you died a little on the inside. How could you not see that their hands were tied? *They were trying to save themselves*, the professor implied, *there was nothing they could do to assist adjuncts*. In the same session, another professor complained about the tone of contingent laborers. "We" were resentful and angry. We shouldn't target the tenured or tenure-track faculty. We should be allies with faculty who claim to be powerless to assist us. You noted that this professor thinks you are a part of that "we" even though you haven't been a lecturer for two and half years. You ask yourself: Why *are* you still here?

Maybe what ultimately convinced you to leave this debate is that you are dead tired of arguing with the tenured over the basic facts of contingent labor in academe. Contingency—you say again and again with a sweet smile that starts to sour—is the norm. You point to data. You explain patiently for the 1,000th time that contingency is not a new problem but one that has been on the rise since the late 1970s. You direct folks to PrecariCorps and its handy chart showing the increase in contingent contracts, or to the AAUP documents warning about this trend years ago. You notice eyes glazing over and fidgety hands. These people don't want to believe you. They are too attached to the notion that faculty hiring is based on merit. You want to smash that notion with a hammer—repeatedly, until there's nothing left but dust.

As you are looking for your exit, the association task force carries on. Its name changes again and again. Plans are made. Plans are accomplished. There's now a travel fund for contingent faculty and graduate students—$500 to attend the annual meeting—that didn't exist in your learned society before. It is a start. There are multiple panels on contingency with growing audiences as each year passes by. The staff of the learned society care deeply about contingency and so does the task force. This is crucial. The work of the task force is raising awareness. You are worried that awareness will not transition into action. You aren't sure this effort is enough.

You aren't sure this is enough because the learned society already had a committee working on a best-practices-for-contingent-faculty document before your task force was created. That first committee contained no contingent faculty. You feel like an asshole when you point that out. The task force reads and comments on a draft of the committee's document. Suggestions are made. Suggestions are accepted. The proposed document is not very radical but falls in line with the best-practice statements from other learned societies. It feels like a solid step in the right direction.

Then the document goes up for review by the association's executive board—and things start to become strange. You get left out of phone calls and emails. Finally, you are included on a call and the executive director and the president of the learned society express concerns over the document's ability to pass the full board. They want to revise it before the board sees it. You and another member of the task force push them to present the document to the board as is—to give the document a chance to pass. The board sends the document to a subcommittee for revisions and your presence is requested. You agree to attend because you try to be agreeable in life. You suddenly remember that part of the reason you were glad to leave academia is that you no longer had to be on committees or attend their meetings. You are obviously doing this post-academic life wrong.

There are phone meetings, so many meetings, to revise the document. These calls convince you that purgatory is an actual place that you inhabit one call at a time. Best practices, you learn, is a controversial term, and things go downhill from there. The administrators (and former administrators) on the subcommittee want to create a document that imagines the problem of contingency from the perspective of chairs and deans. You disagree. You fight over language. You might find yourself banging your head (hard) on the dining-room table that functions as a makeshift desk. Battles are won. Battles are lost.

The document becomes even less radical. It is supposedly a document everyone on the subcommittee can live with. You aren't sure you can. It is mediocre and toothless. It passes the board. The executive leadership is proud; you are angry. People congratulate you for your hard work; you have nothing nice to say in response, so you say nothing at all. You kind of want to pretend you were never involved.

After the document passes, you receive a jovial email from the president of the learned society asking if the work of the task force is done. This email shocks and infuriates you. The task force appears to you as a dog and pony show, after all. Did the president and executive director only want a document? You hope not. You predicted this outcome, which only makes you angrier. You also refuse to let the leadership get away this easily. A document, especially *this* document, can't solve contingency, but other initiatives might force—um, convince—the leadership to take this issue seriously. You stay on, even as you are ready to go.

You can't leave yet because the hard work has just begun, so you'll delay your exit a little while longer. Maybe you aren't quite ready to leave at all.

And then, suddenly, you realize that you are. You resign via email with vague excuses about other interests and new directions. These excuses hold partial truths, but ignore the real reason you can't do it any longer: You are bone-weary of discussing contingency with people who refuse to listen. So, you leave with a whimper rather than a bang.

APRIL 2016

25

WAITING

I'm waiting to hear if I was accepted into an M.F.A. program. Former students, whom I wrote recommendations for, received their acceptances in December and February. I'm still waiting. As each day passes, I dwell on the status of my application. I wonder if maybe the admissions committee passed on me. Maybe my application wasn't strong. Maybe my writing sample struck the wrong chord. Maybe they don't want to accept a 35-year-old freelance writer when they can accept promising writers in their early 20s. Maybe, maybe, maybe. In the absence of knowing, my mind rushes to the worst possible scenario, rejection, not the best possible one, acceptance. Anxiety bubbles to the surface, and I tamp it back down. I still wait.

I'm waiting for my older dog, Hannah, to die. She's a Lab Basset mix, and she's been my companion since she was a puppy and I was a junior in college. Her little legs were so short that her tummy brushed the ground. I only have one photo of her as a puppy, which now seems like a terrible oversight, a mistake I can't remedy. In the fall, we found a tumor on her back and feared that she might have cancer. Countless tests later, the veterinarian explained that it wasn't cancer, and he wasn't sure what actually was ailing her. He was excited to figure it out. I was less so. I waited for tests to come back. I worried about her health. I couldn't face the possibility of her absence. That she, like all other living things, would die. Not my dog, not my Hannah. She recovered as quickly as an old dog could. She lost her hearing a few years ago, and now, she has whatever dementia is for dogs. She doesn't quite know where she is, so she laps our downstairs until sleep overtakes her. She paces in our yard. I watch her and wait for her to get better or worse. She remains the same. That somehow seems worse.

On Sunday, we noticed that she was walking stiffly and appeared to be in pain. Chris set up an appointment for Wednesday, and we waited. On Wednesday, she either had a seizure or a low-blood pressure episode (the vet is unsure which until he runs more tests). She shifted from standing to falling in seconds. Her pained moan rent my heart. It happened again this morning. The kids want to know if she's going to be okay. "I hope so," I say and plaster a fake smile on my face. "I hope so" is the best I can do. The vet assures us that her quality of life is good, but now, he notes, she's blind in one eye. I'm again waiting for her blood tests to return. I'm waiting for a fuller diagnosis. I'm waiting for delay, a reprieve maybe. I'm waiting for her to live while I'm terrified that she's going to die soon. I'm not ready, but she might be. I still wait and watch her.

I'm waiting for something every day. An essay to be

published. A response to an email. A call to be returned. A text message. A child to get ready for school. A child to get ready for preschool. A child to do homework. A child to be potty-trained. A partner to be done with work. A cat to cuddle in my lap. A dog to snore on the porch. An older dog to rest and be well. A child to be well. Another task to be completed.

I wait on laundry to be dry, a pot of water to boil, and a dishwasher to run. I wait as I figure out essays and article assignments. I wait as I try to figure out how to write a book again, another book so different from the others. I find myself waiting on things, small and large. Things that don't matter, and things that matter too much.

I used to hate waiting, but now, I wonder if waiting is where living resides. As we wait, lives begin, lives continue, and lives end. We wait beside each other for things to happen, things to fall apart, or for things to stumble along. We wait and wait and wait.

Waiting is what we do. Maybe waiting makes us who we are. Or maybe the uncertainty of the wait makes us find out who we really are. Maybe we can only know ourselves in the moments between. Maybe the wait teaches us that certainty is never assured. Waiting makes up a majority of our living, so how can I hate it?

This morning, I'm waiting to go on a field trip with my first grader. Her class is headed to a nearby wildlife preserve, and she can't wait. She woke up early this morning (and so did her brother). "I can't wait," she tells me for the 100th time. "I know," I tell her, "I can't either." But, we do wait. I took her brother to preschool and her to school. She has to wait in her classroom until the bus is ready for almost 40 first graders to climb on board. I wait at Starbucks knocking back coffee as if my life depended on it. While I wait, I write to all of you about waiting, which seems more meta than even I can manage. And yet, I do manage it anyway.

My daughter and I will both wait until the wait is over. Waiting makes us more excited for what happens next. Sometimes, waiting primes us for the best possibilities, not the worst. Her field trip was worth waiting for.

I'll continue to wait for news, good or bad. I'll live and wait. Wait and live. I wait in the uncertainty because that is all can do. Often, that's our only option.

MARCH 2016

THE MEN WHO EMAIL ME

As I was driving home today from dropping off children at school and preschool, my mind drifted to the men who email me about my writing. I'm not quite sure why I decided to think about those men, whom I've never met but who chose to contact me anyway. Perhaps I thought about them because of the discussions surrounding the #MoreThanMean video, in which men were asked to read harassing tweets sent to female sports writers. The catch was that the men had to read the tweets out loud sitting face-to-face with the writers. Some of the men found themselves unable to say aloud what was tweeted. The #MoreThanMean campaign hopes to bring attention to the online harassment of women in sports.

Of course, online harassment is not just a problem for women who write about sports, but for women who write about anything (and women on the Internet more generally). I know that factually as well as intimately because it has happened to me.

In 2007, I started blogging for Religion in American History. When I began writing more about racial violence and white supremacy, commenters were not nice. A commenter actually threatened my life when I wrote about the murder of George Tiller. I shrugged off the threat; Chris did not. After my book was published in 2011, I started receiving emails from men who read my work and expected me to respond to their criticisms. A "Son of the Confederacy" emailed to let me know how wrong I was about Nathan Bedford Forrest being a Klansman and accused me of harming his legacy. A man claiming to be the "Second Coming of Jesus" wrote me a letter, in which he called me "honey" and told me that I was wrong about the Klan, race, religion, and well, everything. If I only would visit him at his home, he would explain what was really happening in the world. I declined and laughed off the letter, but a member of my department told me to contact the FBI.

On the Facebook page I created for my book, *Gospel According to the Klan*, men have called me a racist, threatened to beat my ass, and promised to hunt me down and show me how wrong my racism is. None of those men seemed to recognize that I'm a historian who studies the Klan, not a member of the order. I took screenshots of their messages and reported them to Facebook. I tried to find humor in the situation.

The emails and messages were anomalies in my life that I tried to make into funny stories about the weirdness of being a scholar in the Internet age. When freelance writing became my career, the messages were no longer anomalies but constant realities. I'm a woman who writes on the Internet, which means men email me to tell me what they think of what I've written whether I want to know or not. My attempts to find humor in the ugliness are long gone.

This morning, I found myself thinking about all these men, who are strangers to me, and the routine similarity of their emails in tone, style, and content.

The men who email me tell me that I'm wrong. I've made the wrong argument. I've missed the essential issue or the salient details. I've made errors and mistakes. I didn't use data. I used too much data. They assert that gender is not as big of an issue as I make it out to be or that I don't realize how hard it is to be a man. They assert that I can never be anything but wrong.

The men who email me claim that I don't know anything about higher education, religious studies, labor, gender, or any other topic on which I've ever written an essay. They ignore my credentials in favor of assuming my incompetency. "You didn't possibly think this through," they type. They don't care that I have—they just assume that I haven't. If competency appears out of reach, expertise becomes impossible.

The men who email me explain that I haven't considered the consequences of what I write. They want me to know that I've opened the door to critiques of academia from "The Right" or "Rightists" (their language, not mine). My essays give ammunition to all of those conservatives who despise higher education. I become singularly responsible for academia's downfall. I wonder when I became so powerful without realizing it.

The men who email me sometimes start with a compliment about how much they "enjoyed" my essay. Then, they proceed to send me their own writing on the subject and tell me to "please include it" next time because they are experts on the topic. They are *the* experts. How did I not know that? Their emails are just remedying the situation and improving my knowledge. In pointing to their own writing, they claim to have a revolutionary work that will vastly enhance anything that I am writing. They view themselves as epic poets, should-have-been-famous scholars, and amazing-but-unrecognized authors. They haven't read a word I've written, but they expect me to hang on every word of theirs.

The men who email me need me to know that *they took the time to read my writing.* They paused in their busy day to read 1,000 words of mine, which they somehow assume makes me indebted to them. A writer is beholden to the reader, right? They read my essay, so I must respond to whatever they email—no matter how demeaning or awful. I think they misunderstand a writer's obligations.

The men who email me demand to know why I didn't get an academic job and why I left academia. They want me to tell them what went wrong in every excruciating detail. They want me to justify the life choices I made without acknowledging how those choices were forced. They want me to justify my continued existence. They want me to go away.

The men who email me insult the content and style of my writing. They need me to know that I'm a terrible writer who doesn't deserve a platform. How did I get to write for these publications anyway? Why didn't these publications recruit *them?*

The men who email me ask for favors. They read my essays,

so why won't I read, edit, and comment on theirs? These men expect my labor for free. They expect me to help. They want my advice. In fact, I did read and edit a few essays from men I didn't know. Once I gave them feedback or advice, they never emailed again.

The men who email me beg me to promote their work. They just wrote *the best essay ever,* and I should share, um, they mean, read it. And then share it. For them. To be helpful. They don't like to take "no" for an answer. I learned to say "no" anyway.

The men who email me are not anonymous. They use their personal or work email accounts. They gladly offer their names, their job titles, and their sense of entitlement. They can't imagine that I would refuse to listen to them. It is just an email, just a comment, just a criticism, or just a threat—what's my problem?

The men who email me take up space in my inbox. They take up space in my head. They take up my time. What amazes me is that these men think that I owe *them* time, attention, and effort because they read something I wrote. I don't owe them anything, but I seem to be the only one who knows that. These men continue to believe that I deserve their opinions. I want them to learn to keep their opinions to themselves.

Last week, I decided against writing an essay I had pitched about bros in academia. I struggled to write the piece because I could not deal with the prospect of more of these men emailing me. I could not face yet another dumpster fire in my inbox. I weighed the impact of the essay's possible reception against my mental well-being, and I killed it because I knew I wouldn't be able to manage the nasty responses. Some weeks, I can ignore what the men who email me say. Last week was not one of those. My essay died a quiet death, and my inbox remained uneventful.

What you need to know is that the harassment I face is mild compared to what other women writers have experienced. *It could be so much worse*, I tell myself—as if that makes anything better. Mild harassment is still harassment.

I've stopped reading the emails from these men. I might read a first line. I might toss Chris my phone and ask him to read the email. He will delete it for me. I stopped reading their essays. I stopped offering advice and sharing their work. I stopped giving justifications. I stopped responding to them. I stopped interacting with the men who email me because I don't have to explain myself, or my work, to them. No matter what they might think, they aren't entitled to my explanations, time, or effort.

And still, men email me to ask me for favors, explanations, and justifications. They continue to think that reading my work gives them the right to my time and attention. I no longer grant them either.

Finally, I learned that I didn't have to respond. And you don't, either.

MAY 2016

ON REJECTION

In 2012, I was on the Metro riding away from the annual meeting of American Academy of Religion, and for once, I felt hopeful. I had a few conference interviews, but one particular interview went remarkably well. I was finally on the path to getting that tenure-track job that I wanted so desperately. Everyone keep telling me that this was my year, and I started to believe them. My phone buzzed to let me know I received an email from the search chair of my remarkable interview. I wavered on whether to click on it or not.

My fate to be determined by a one paragraph.

The chair informed me that I would not be receiving a campus visit and wished me luck of the rest of my job search.

I was stunned. Another rejection to add to my mounting pile of job rejections. I was once again an academic failure. I wasn't sure that I would recover. As the train inched closer to the airport, my hurt and bafflement turned to anger. I was angry at the search committee, the search chair, my advisor, and everyone who assured me I would succeed. I hadn't succeeded, had I?

Then, I did a quick tally of my successes: a book contract that turned into a published book, journal articles, book chapters, panels that I organized, and papers I had given. Basically, I realized that I had done everything academia asked of me and still I felt like a failure. Maybe, the academia version of success was screwed up. Maybe, I couldn't succeed if success was narrowly tied to the kind of employment I had. Maybe, rejection wasn't failure, but something else entirely.

When my anger dissipated, I realized, not for the first time, that academia wasn't for me, and more importantly, that I could survive that realization and likely thrive. I wouldn't let rejection define me any longer than I already had. What I know now, over four years later, is that I learned more about myself and higher education from those rejected job applications than I ever did from my successes. Rejection forced me to find another career and another way to live in this world. Rejection opened me up to possibilities I never would have imagined and allowed me space to recognize that academia was only a part of my world, not the defining feature. Rejection made me a more determined scholar and allowed me to become a writer. It changed my path in ways that I appreciate more and more every passing day. Rejection was never actually a failure, but a new possibility.

MAY 2016

WHAT REJECTION FEELS LIKE

Last week, my editor from *Vitae* asked me to write a few paragraphs about rejection and failure in academia for a feature. The goal was to have a variety of contributors discuss how we've experienced and dealt with rejection as well as what we've learned. I wasn't quite sure what I wanted to write. Rejection is not fun, even when you are used to it. (And writers have to get used to it.) I don't tend to handle it very well, so I'm not the best role model. Additionally, there are still people who consider me an academic failure, who don't seem to care that I, and many others, abandoned the narrow academic view of success awhile ago. I worried over what to say.

When I told Chris about the feature, he noted, "You're going to tell them you handle rejection with bourbon and CW shows, right?"

"Probably not," I replied, "but maybe I should."

On Monday, I decided to write about a hard and swift rejection for a tenure-track job in 2012. Back then, I was actively seeking a tenure-track job, and this particular position was one that I desperately wanted. This rejection forced me to realize—not for the first time—that academia might not be the place for me. Also, it was a safe to write about a rejection from almost four years ago. It wasn't a recent brush with failure, but one that I had long come to terms with. I could write about rejection, and perhaps, not be bothered by it.

Someone asked me recently how I felt about not attaining the job I trained for and dreamed of. If she had asked me three years ago, I would have burst into tears and collapsed on the floor. If she had asked me two years ago, my rage would have consumed me. If she had asked me a year ago, I would have binge-watched shows on Netflix rather than answer her question. My response to her, instead, was reserved, calm even. I considered my failed academic career and found that I'm not overwhelmed by anger, sadness, and frustration. The path that came to a dead end no longer wounds me. There's still an occasional twinge of disappointment and a whole lot of anger about higher education's reliance on contingent workers, but I'm okay. I survived the end of one dream and moved on to others.

I channeled my survival and okayness into my reflections on rejection. Rejection was not the failure I assumed it to be, but a possibility, a forceful nudge onto another path I hadn't quite considered. I was happy to realize that I could view rejection in such a positive light. Once I knew I survived this rejection and so many others, I could see how rejection allowed me to become a different person than I imagined I would be. A better person.

On Tuesday, I received an email about the status of my M.F.A. application, which required me to click on a link to a website, log in, and navigate two more pages before my status was revealed. My application was rejected. I had received an earlier email about being wait-listed, but now, I had proof that I wouldn't be starting an M.F.A. in the fall semester. I was again rejected. Another dream dismissed.

I had forgotten how rejection feels in the moment. A sucker punch to the gut that leaves you gasping for air and doubled over. A door that previously seemed ajar is slammed in your face. A floor that disappears from beneath your feet while you flail on your descent to the ground. Yet-another-opportunity passes you by, but body checks you hard on the way out.

I felt hollow, bruised, and weary. I had put myself out there by applying. I started to have hope. I dreamed another dream, and all I found was familiar rejection and the feelings of being (once again) a failure.

I bumbled through Tuesday and Wednesday trying not to dwell in my own misery, but unable to stop myself. "This hit me harder than I expected," I tell Chris. He gives me a hug. Usually, I would try to ignore the rejection and stay busy, but I leaned into my disappointment, upset, and angry. I chose to mourn what could have been. I allowed myself to feel what I felt without judgment or derision.

And I started to feel better. By Thursday, something shifted as it always does after a rejection. Hurt transformed into determination. Standing in front of my computer, I reminded myself that a rejection to an M.F.A. program doesn't make me less of a writer. It could have been a nice adventure, but it didn't happen. I'll keep writing anyway.

The rejection spurred me to pull together the essays I've

already written on endings. I'm creating a collection of essays on endings and apocalypses. What I found surprised me: I had already written four essays on the theme without quite intending to, and there are so many more I yearn to write. I keep wanting to write this book, but seem to put it off month after month because of assignments, small children, and life more generally.

I need to write this book, so I decide that the time is now.

Rejection gave me the clarity I'd been seeking about my writing and work, but wasn't quite ready for. It forced me to think deeply about why I write and what I write. It pushed me to another a path created by my own hands, not someone else's.

It hurt. (It always hurts.) But, rejection was never a failure, just another possibility.

MAY 2016

29

DEAR SUGAR...

I find my thoughts turning to Cheryl Strayed. Again.

On Facebook, a friend of mine noted, "writing is hard," and instantly, I shared one of my favorite Strayed essays, "Write Like A Motherfucker," with him. *Writing is hard*, she reminds us, *other things, like coal mining, are harder.* As I walked Zan yesterday, I kept thinking "the fuck is your life, Kelly, so what are you going to do with it?" Above my desk hangs a large Dear Sugar poster, which chides me about giving up and suggests I employ the remarkable power of "no." On my right arm, I have "be brave enough" tattooed on my forearm. Those three words are the start of some of Strayed's most powerful advice: "Be brave enough to break your own heart." Your life, my life, is too important to be held back by the possibility of heartbreak. I hold her words tightly; I'll never let them go.

Strayed's words come to mind when I begin to evaluate my path, my career, or my life.

As you probably guessed, I'm a serious fan of Strayed. I've

read her *Tiny Beautiful Things*, the collection of her Dear Sugar columns for *The Rumpus*, again and again and again. Her gracious, gritty, and humane advice helped me consider the life I was building when I was unsure what I wanted my life to be. I left behind one career with no real plan for another. I had two children rather than one child. I moved from Tennessee back to Florida. The world was shifting out from under me, and I had no idea when or where I might land. Frankly, I was terrified. In this time of upheaval, I found her Dear Sugar columns and then promptly bought her book. Her advice changed my life. Perhaps, it saved my life.

I still return to her writing when feel the ground shifting yet again. Yet this time, there's nothing quite so cataclysmic. It's the ordinary and expected changes that are putting me off balance. The world moves forward, and I'm trying hard to keep up. Some days, I fear I won't be able to.

My daughter finished first grade today. She'll start second grade in August. This fact gives me pause. Day by day, she's shedding the remnants of her early life as a baby and toddler. If I look at her from the right angle, I get glimpses of the young woman she'll become. Her curious dark-hazel eyes are reminiscent of my own, but startlingly different. She's learning to be her own person, whom I'm eager to meet but not quite yet.

A few weeks ago, my son grew a couple inches taller. His shorts finally inched above his knees rather than below. He'll be three in September, and he no longer looks much like the chubby baby he used to be. He's a toddler transforming into a little boy. Again, I feel that I'm at a loss. Soon, he'll be too big for me to rock him. My heart will break just a little at the transition. I must be brave enough to let them grow and, eventually, go.

I want to stop everything. I want to watch them grow in painstaking detail. I'm not ready for their transitions because I'm rarely ready for my own.

And I feel, yet again, that I'm on the edge of another transition, or maybe, their transitions are forcing me to transform with them. (I hate transitions. I'm not sure I'm ready for another transformation.)

But, I'm unsure what this transition is; I feel uneasy. Something is about to change for me, but I'm not ready to recognize what it is. The world is shifting again, but incrementally. Part of me wants to escape into novels and television until the feeling passes. The more sensible part of me realizes that escaping is not engaging. I need to be engaged. I need to build my life rather than let others build it for me. I need to build a life no matter what the transitions are. Life is about how we weather our transitions. We can cling to the way we want the world to be or we can be open to possibilities. We can choose to grow. Or we can choose not to.

I pick up *Tiny Beautiful Things* again and wait for the transition. I need to be ready for what happens next, and Strayed's advice soothes my unease.

If I can only remember to be brave enough, I'll be okay.

MAY 2016

30

GIG

In June, I applied for a new gig. An editor position became available for a publication I liked. I wasn't actively looking for a job, but an opportunity appeared. It seemed foolish to not pay attention, so I did.

I appeared as the shoo-in. The current editor recommended me to the higher up; the higher up seemed interested in me. After tidying up my résumé and crafting a narrative of my work history in writing and publishing, I did a phone interview, which went well. The interviewer mentioned shifts in the company that might change the way operations worked. I was offered the gig anyway, so I accepted it.

Weeks passed. I hadn't received a contract or a confirmation of the salary or a start date. I emailed. The higher up promised soon. I emailed more. Assurances piled up. Still no contract. All I had was a verbal agreement and emails that made promises. I felt something was wrong.

I chose to ignore that feeling because I was excited. This gig would be a well-paying one. I could cut back some of my paid writing and focus more on my collection of essays. It was remote work with a schedule that fit around my children's school and preschool schedules. I started to make plans. We could pay off student loans, put money away for retirement, or whatever. Finally, I would have a salary that could cover our family's expenses if something went wrong with my partner's job. Instead of the quilt of gigs and assignments that I've patched together over the last three years, I would have a contract that paid me monthly for at least two years. I would have a day job that allowed me to do the writing I wanted on my own terms rather than the balancing (not-really balancing) act that exists now.

To be honest, the rejection from the M.F.A. got under my skin in ways that I didn't fully realize. I doubted my ability to write. I doubted myself. Yes, I managed to get essays off to an agent who's interested in my work, but the doubt settled on me. It was a weight I couldn't shake off. I don't know why I was rejected from the M.F.A., but my brain reached desperately for explanations in the absence of knowledge. Maybe, I didn't want it enough, and it showed. Maybe, I was too old to have that shimmery gloss of potential that young writers exude from their pores. Maybe, the admissions committee found my writing uninspired, rote, or pedestrian. Maybe, my essays were not literary enough. Maybe, my writing would never be literary enough. Maybe, my ideas were bad. Maybe, I wasn't imaginative enough. Maybe, maybe, maybe....

Maybe, I wasn't cut out to be a writer. This last explanation knocked me off my feet. It caught traction, and I couldn't get it to go away. It became a drumbeat that resounded in my bones for days, weeks, and months.

My writing slowed down. I managed to scrape together assignments, but writing no longer brought me the joy it once had. I turned to books I love for inspiration. I came away wanting. I wrote about what editors assigned. I didn't want to do more. I couldn't do more.

This gig became the easy route to leaving writing behind. I would become an editor. I would write or not write. Who cares? Life would move on. I pinned my hopes on this new gig because I had to pin them somewhere. I leaned heavily on this hope. I needed it to bear my weight. I wasn't sure it could.

This week, I emailed the higher up again about my contract for the gig. The email I received was odd and directed me to contact two other higher ups about the position. I emailed them. They emailed back that the position was being re-imagined with a new job description that they helpfully attached to the email. The gig that was once mine was no longer. I quickly looked over the new description. My heart sank. They changed the qualifications, and I felt I could no longer apply. More than that, I was unsure I even wanted the job that was now listed.

A few minutes later, I received a rejection on an essay that's been under review by a literary magazine for four months. The universe seemed to be telling me something. Lucky for me, I don't believe the universe cares that much about my existence. Otherwise, it would appear that the universe wanted to kick me in the teeth.

I was furious and sad and miserable. But, I wasn't shocked. I already suspected something was amiss with the gig. I already imagined that I would receive a rejection for this particular magazine. Still, both rejections hurt. (As rejections always do.)

"I shouldn't have gotten my hopes up," I uttered to Chris. But, I didn't really mean it. I refuse to not get my hopes up, even if it means that my heart will be broken again and again. Hope is about possibilities. I need to live in a world of possibility.

Something strange happened. This lost gig made my thoughts turn to writing. To evaluate my writing career, ponder what I want it to be, and discover how I'm going to get there.

I recognized some truths that have been waiting patiently for my attention to turn to them. I've been sending my essays to the wrong kinds of magazines. I was taking this gig, even though I was nervous about what it would mean for my larger writing projects. I want to write about endings and apocalypses on my own timeframe rather than someone else's. I'm tired of writing about higher education just because people think I should write about it. What inspires me to write now is different from what inspired me to start freelance writing career. I want to edit more because I like helping other writers make their work better. I still define myself by other people's definitions of success to my detriment.

Rejection always makes me refocus on what's important. It's the reality check I need, but not that I want. There are always more lessons to learn. When we stop learning from missteps, rejections, and losses, we stop growing as people. Personal growth often hurts, but it is oh-so-necessary.

I now have different plans: applying to nonfiction prizes, new journals to submit my work, and the renewed desire to write what matters to me. I also received another gig, an unexpected one. I keep writing because I can't seem to make myself stop.

One door closes, but the doors that remain open are the ones I seek.

JULY 2016

On August 15th, another birthday passed, and I turned 36. It was the first day of school for my now-second grader. It was the beginning of the third week in a new classroom for my toddler. Chris and I took them to preschool and then school, and we had a morning together without small children in tow. I had a birthday (almond-milk) latte at a new coffee shop named Lucky Goat. We wandered from shop to shop. We bought the kids some new books at the bookstore. We had lunch with gluten-free French fries, which are much harder to find than they should be.

Months ago, I promised myself that if I still wanted to that I would get my septum pierced for my 36th birthday, so I did. I almost backed out at the last possible moment as the needle rested against the fragile skin of the inside of my nose, but I didn't. I now have silver horseshoe peeking out of both of my nostrils. I can't help but love how it looks. It gives me an edge that I didn't know I needed. As we got back into the car, I told Chris, "I look like a badass," and I can't help but grin. Rebellion, I've learned, is not something I'm going to easily outgrow. It's an old friend that I refuse to leave behind.

Later when Chris had to phone in to a work meeting, I read fiction and drank more coffee. I picked the kids up, and they wished me happy birthday again. They gave me hugs and kisses. They sang a version of "Happy Birthday" in which I lived in a zoo and looked like I was 102 before dissolving into giggles. It was a lovely day, a truly lovely birthday. 36 was off to an excellent start.

And it needed to be. I needed a lovely day. Frankly, I needed more than one.

35 turned out to be a hard year for me: newly uncovered food allergies, multiple job rejections, a rejection from an M.F.A. program, my fifteen-year-old dog died, and the other smaller disasters that hardly register but leave a fierce mark that still sting if you manage to touch them.

For much of 35, I wondered what I was doing with my life. Where I was headed? What did I really want? There were more transitions than I expected on the horizon, and I was already weary of transitions. I realized that I lacked a real plan, so I started to plan. My plans failed, so I planned some more. More plans failed. I threw myself at opportunities. They didn't pan out. A person can only handle so much rejection in any given period of time. I found myself exhausted, burned out, and spent. And then, the summer hit hard, and the funk that I hoped was lifting seemed determined to stay. I started to hate everything. I hated writing. I hated other writers. I hated our new summer schedule. I hated the expectations that other people placed on me. I hated myself and my inability to move past the rejections, the losses, and the grievances. Everything chafed and frustrated me.

"I didn't sign up for any of this," I texted a friend after a particularly trying day of parenting and not-writing.

I didn't sign up for any of this, I told myself, *again and again and again*. I didn't sign up for any of it. I wasn't sure I wanted to be a part-time writer while mothering two children. I wasn't sure that I didn't want to be a writing mama either. I wasn't sure I could give up writing if I tried. I wasn't sure whether I wanted to look for different jobs. I wasn't sure what jobs to look for. I wasn't sure I wanted to anything beyond what I currently had. I wasn't sure what I wanted at all.

What life did I want instead? I had no answer for that either. I just knew that something wasn't quite working, but I wasn't sure how to fix it. So, I decided to not fix anything, but to move forward simply because I didn't want to. One foot in front of the other to move away from my funk and into a healthier, happier space. I find it so easy to slip into negativity rather than find the perspective that I really need.

I decided to think no longer of what opportunities I missed out on at 35, but what I still had. I still had my writing. I was still writing essays. I even curated and edited my own series of essays on music. I now have over 23,000 words on a manuscript that will become a collection of essays someday (but not necessarily soon). I have a faithful dog and a faithful but surly cat. I have two loving, albeit exhausting, children. I have a partner who loves me even when I can't find any love for myself. I have friends and colleagues and mentors and tweeps. My family still loves me even if I decided to get my septum pierced at 36. I'm loved, and I love all of these people, which is kind of wonderful and awe-inspiring when you stop to think about it. I had another year on this remarkably messed up, but beautiful planet. Others were not quite so lucky.

35 could have been so much worse, but it wasn't.

And now, at the start of another year, I'm determined not to waste it. I'm going to work for hard for the lovely days. I hope you will too.

AUGUST 2016

32

NOT LUCKY

Within the first two weeks of being 36, I learned that my first book, *Gospel According to the Klan*, would become a paperback edition, and I was offered the position as editor of *Women in Higher Education*.

My luck, which was not great before, seemed to be turning around.

Finally, I had good news. The book that I worked hard to create gets a longer shelf life than I imagined it would (and an eBook edition, too). And I now had a day job that pays a good salary. After three years of working as a freelancer, in which I often had to fight with people to get paid weeks or months after my articles were published, I get paid the same week of every month. Moreover, being editor is a job that I love, complete with new challenges, clear expectations, and a remarkable about of email. Each month I know what I need to accomplish with a clear deadline, and I still get to write.

At first, I felt lucky. I was moving forward instead of

treading the same stale water day in and day out. I no longer had to scramble to write.

Yet, luck is just one way to narrate the story: to make it about coincidence and things coming together when I least expected it. I imagined all was lost, but it wasn't! The universe didn't hate me! (Perhaps, the universe needed to teach me the importance of patience and waiting, which makes me think the universe might actually be ambivalent about me. Patience is not my strong suit.) Finally, things were looking up!

Luck is probably the most convenient and simplest way to narrate these events, but that doesn't make it true. The story ends with successes (I have a job!), but ignores all the work and struggle that goes into both our successes and failures. Luck obscures the work that we do to make future opportunities possible.

To say I was lucky, ignores that my book sold enough copies to qualify for a paperback. Ignores the years that I spent researching, writing, revising, polishing, and ultimately, creating that book. Ignores that instructors and professors still assign this book for their classes to read. Ignores that people still continue to read it. Ignores that I still write about the Klan and the order's relevance to contemporary politics. Ignores that this book was made of effort, tears, and sweat.

To say I was lucky, ignores that I've been writing about gender and higher education for three years. Ignores that I've spent more hours than I could keep track of researching, analyzing, and writing about how sexism is part of the structure of academia. Ignores all the studies I've read, all the words I've written, and all the work that goes into becoming an expert on a topic outside my field of study (even if I'm not entirely sure I can be expert outside what I trained for). Ignores that I try to become an expert anyway. Ignores all the successful and failed pitches, the most-shared articles, the ones that everyone seemed to ignore, and the articles that I began to write but just couldn't finish. Ignores the toil that writing about the sexism beat takes on me, but also my commitment to smashing the patriarchy word by word, paragraph by paragraph, and article by article. Ignores that I wrote for *Women in Higher Education* for two years.

To say I'm lucky, ignores that the crafting of resumes and other interview materials. Ignores the interview (and all the other interviews before it). Ignores the blind panic of putting my fate in another person's hands when I applied for the job. Ignores the stress of applying for this job after I applied for so many others that only ended in rejection. Ignores the vulnerable hope that I had to craft to convince myself that this job might be different from all the others. Ignores the stress of waiting, the assumption of failure, and the preemptive dejected posture that my body seemed to take. Ignores that I really wanted this job, but I couldn't let myself want it too much because the possible rejection would hurt more. Ignores the joy of the job offer and the new panic of whether I would learn what I should to become a good editor.

To tell a story about luck is to tell a story shorn of the work, emotions, and disquiet of the last three years.

Luck removes my agency from the story to make everything look tidy, rather than narrating that I was most often a hot mess trying to create a space in the world and seeking a career different from the one I left behind. Luck doesn't tell anyone about the days I spent watching Netflix and gorging on potato chips or the days that getting out of bed was the hardest task on my to-do list.

Luck ignores and obscures. Luck hides the story of our struggles to where we are going. It's an easier narration. It's the one you expect to hear, which makes me want to refuse it even more. Luck ignores the hard middle of our stories and offers up shallowest narration.

So, I've been attempting to narrate this story of recent successes as one of work and emotions rather than luck. I'll admit that there's some luck involved in the story of how I went from academic to writer to editor and still writer, but luck is only apparent in glimmers. There's also networking, tweeting, and a serious amount of clean copy too. But mostly, there's work, sometimes easy, sometimes hard, not luck. Work to create enough articles to call myself a writer. Work to edit enough articles to call myself editor. Work to convince myself to do the work day after day when rejection was all I seemed to face. Work to remain a person in this world. Work to keep moving forward. Work to try again and again and again. Work to not give up.

Sometimes, our work pays off. It's just hard to know what will pay off when we're in the struggle.

I wasn't lucky, even if I still kind of feel that way. I refuse to give luck all of the credit. Maybe you shouldn't either.

OCTOBER 2016

33

MOVING FORWARD

On a whim, I got another tattoo. I happened to be in San Antonio covering a conference. I happened to want a tattoo. There happened to be a custom shop half a mile from my hotel. I took this as a sign, so I walked over and waited at the front of the shop with its skulls, its portraits of Mary and Jesus, and its turquoise blue walls.

I decided on a delicate arrow to grace the side of my left hand. The tattoo artist sketched up the arrow in about two minutes. The stencil was on, and then, about 10 minutes later, he slathered on A&D and wrapped up my hand in Saran wrap and Scotch tape. Getting the tattoo barely hurt (when compared to all of the other tattoos that I have that took hours and hours to complete). My skin turned pink and puffy afterwards, a delayed reaction to the sting of the needle and black ink embedded in my flesh.

While I type, the arrow points forward. That was not an accident. I wanted a tattoo to remind me to move forward. I needed something to remind me to put one foot in front of the other. To move and to look forward.

I was inspired by Blair Braverman's recent essay, "What Dogs Can Teach Us About Persistence," a lovely reflection that begins with Brewtus, her lead sled dog, realizing that he can U-turn.[1] This is a disaster because the dogs need to move only forward. Most of her dogs, however, are inclined to head in the right direction. She writes, "No matter where the dogs are, there is only one direction, and it is forward. No matter what they face, there is only one way, and it is through."

First, I read her essay quickly because of fierce desire to know where it was going to end. And then, I read it slowly savoring what Braverman says about persistence of both dogs and people and the need to move through. Then, I read it again and again. She writes, "Dogs carry wounds, but they don't carry the past." This line made me cry at every rereading. Dogs carry wounds, but they don't carry the past. *If only*, I thought, *if only people were so lucky.*

These days I feel like I'm jogging in place. I get up each morning, I get kids ready for school and preschool, I pack a lunch for the toddler, I drive them to their respective schools on my mornings, I drink coffee, I answer email, I edit, I drink more coffee, I might walk the dog, I plan issues of *Women in Higher Education*, I maybe convince myself to write, I edit, I email some more, I go to meetings about social justice in our community, I scroll through Twitter, I get furious at the news, I pick up kiddos from preschool and afterschool, I wrangle the oldest to get her to do homework, I make dinner or I scrounge up dinner from leftovers on my nights, I count down to the inevitable bedtimes for children, I check the news even though I know I shouldn't, I spend time with Chris as we watch Netflix, and then I head to bed. The next day is the same and the next and the next and the next. I'm in a holding pattern that I can't quite shake.

My life is routine; our lives are routine.

This is something you might not know about me: I crave routine and schedules. Since I was very small, I wanted to know how each day would play out in exacting order with no deviation from the routine. I want no surprises; I want days to be ordered and routine. And this routine that I described is familiar and comfortable. It's what I'm used to. It's what I wanted for the longest time, a family life different from what I had growing up.

But now, it also feels like I'm stuck. I love my partner, I love my kids, I love my job, but something feels amiss.

It's like the years of pretending to be normal have finally caught up with me. Like all the attempts at running away from the past always fail because I'm stuck with what I experienced. Like I can't run away from myself, even though I have given it a solid go. Like actively avoiding the trauma caused by an emotionally and mentally abusive parent is something that I can no longer quite avoid. Like recognizing that it took me until I was 36 to be able to utter the word "abuse" without falling apart. Like this life I've fought to create needs to finally acknowledge that I survived. Like I have to deal with the past directly if I want to move forward.

What I finally recognized is that dealing with past doesn't mean remaining there. I'm no longer the girl that I was, but I can admire how she fought to survive. I can admire how she saved my life.

People carry wounds, and we also carry the past, whether we want to or not. And that's okay. What I learned from Braverman, and her dogs, is tenacity and persistence of moving through. People can carry the past and move forward with the recognition that we survived and the hope of what awaits us in the distance.

The small arrow is a reminder, a prompt to keep my feet shuffling forward, a reminder to keep trudging through. I can still glimpse back, but I don't have to turn around.

Rereading all of these essays in *Grace Period*, I was actually glad to glimpse back to see how my shift out of academia started and led me to the life I have now. Glimpsing back helped me realize that I have moved forward, and I keep moving forward because none of us can really manage to stand still. Each day contains uncertainty and possibility; there's freedom in that if we're willing to see it. Almost four years later, I feel freer than I did when I first started writing these essays. My ideas about success and failure radically changed by realizing that I have choices about the life that I'm living beyond what other people hand down to me. I've stumbled from one path to another. Sometimes, I land on my face, but other times, I find a different path than the one I was looking for, a better path that I would have missed without the failures and rejections.

Granted, I still have bad days because everyone has bad days. But, I like where I've landed now, and I never want to go back to where I was when I started this gradual exit out of academia. I refuse to turn around. This collection, then, was never about the end of my transition, about where I am now, but a catalog of how transitions *feel* in all of their highs and lows. Mine was not a path of seamless transition from one type of life to another, but rather a string of successes, failures, and upheavals to get to where I am now. My grace period still doesn't quite feel finished because it's my life. And yet, the collection has to end. Sometimes, an ending is an ending, but sometimes it's a place where we stop to rest and reflect before moving on. It's time to move on. It's time to move forward.

Thanks for sharing my journey, and keep moving forward.

APRIL 2017

———

1. Blair Braverman, "What Dogs Teach Us About Persistence," *Outside*, February 23, 2017.

ACKNOWLEDGMENTS

I didn't intend to write this book.

It started out as a blog post that became a column. Then, I wrote another column and another and another. And I wrote other essays about my transition out of academia. I was writing to figure out how my life turned out. I was writing to convince myself that my life, so different than what I imagined, was worth reimagining, changing, and saving. I didn't realize then how important writing this series was to me. I didn't quite comprehend how much my transition from the academy relied on creating a new and different narrative of who I wanted to be —and who I was becoming. I managed to save my life word by word, paragraph by paragraph, and page by page.

On a whim, I mentioned on Twitter pulling together all of my "Grace Period" essays as a collection, and I was surprised by the amount of people who encouraged me to do so. Mostly, I wanted to see what happened when the essays resided side-by-side rather than as disparate essays drifting along on the internet. I was glad to realize that readers, who have followed my journey since my earliest blog post on taking a break from academia, would want to see what happens too. As I started collecting essays from *Chronicle Vitae*, my site, and my TinyLetter and arranging them chronologically, I found that I had written more than I remembered. I had much to say about my feelings in this attempt to build a new life. But, I worried, as I often do, about the essays I gathered. Did they truly belong together? Was I imagining a coherence that wasn't really there? Did anyone care about my feelings or my story?

And yet, as I reread and lightly revised the essays, I recognized that there's something to gain in their togetherness: a portrait of the toil, vulnerability, and hope of a life after dreams falter, stall, and fail. I made it through, reader, you can too.

But, I wouldn't have made it without the enthusiasm, support, camaraderie, and friendship of so many people. I wouldn't have written this book without them, and I'm grateful to have each of them in my life, online and off.

Grace Period would not have existed, as it does now, without Gabriella Montell encouraging me write about my post-academic transition for *Vitae*. Gabriella gave me a column, a platform to speak, about what life was like for so many of us in the academy as contingent laborers. Her desire to hear my story helped me realize that it was worth hearing. I cannot offer her enough thanks for my first freelance writing gig that led to many more. Additionally, Denise Manger edited many of essays you find here that originally appeared at *Vitae*, so she helped make my writing better. Any faults are my own.

Thanks to Brook Wilensky-Lanford, the editor of *Killing the Buddha* and its press, for thinking a collection of essays on transitions and building a life was a worthwhile endeavor. Thanks also to Gordon Haber for creating the eBook and cover. And thanks to Blue Crow Press for believing that *Grace Period* should be a paperback and for convincing me that I should believe it, too. (It didn't take much convincing.)

When I started writing openly about academia, I also found a community of post-ac and alt-ac folks on Twitter, who helped me see that transitions were possible by sharing their own. I'm lucky to call most of these folks my friends. Thanks to Liana Silva, Joe Fruscione, Katie Rose Guest Pryal, Lee Skallerup Bessette, Jen Polk, Elizabeth Keenan, Hussein Rashid, Chuck Pearson, and Josh Eyler. Chuck's joy about this project buoyed me. Joe's support and encouragements to "stay fancy" still cheer me up when I most need it. Liana was first my writing buddy and then a dear friend who eased my worries with texts, hilarious memes and GIFs, and lovely letters about why we write. Not only did Katie read, share, and comment on some of my earliest essays, but she also helped me realize how to end this collection. In the earliest days of my separation from academic life, Betsy Barre shared her journey from one career to another and kept encouraging me to write about my own.

A number of academics were wary of my slow, prolonged exit out of the academy, but others supported me as I became adjacent to academia rather firmly placed than within its confines. Thanks to Megan Goodwin, Shreena Gandhi, Art Remillard, Mike Altman, Russell McCutcheon, Anthea Butler, Emily Clark, Matthew Cressler, David Watt, Laura Levitt,

Amy Koehlinger, Richard Newton, Sean McCloud, Jason Bivins, and Martin Kavka. A special thanks to Martin, a beloved mentor and friend, who quickly became one of my fiercest supporters. He gave me the room to make my own decisions, when I needed that more than anything. Martin, your encouragement means more than you know, so thank you for continuing to support me for years after I was one of your students.

Over coffee dates, Heather Nicholson guided me to the realization that I didn't need to be an academic to ask the big questions that I wanted to ask, but rather there was freedom in creating a career I wanted, not just settling for the one I thought I was supposed to have. Heather, I wished you lived closer, so we could still have coffee. Rachel Christensen first read my essays and then decided we should be friends in transitions. I'm so very glad she did.

My family had to the up-close view of the toll it took to leave behind my career plans. It wasn't pretty, but they continued to love me anyway. Because that's what they do best. For that, I'm grateful to Dottie and Steve Raines; Stephanie, Jerry, Jackson, and Emily Ann Basford; Ashley, Brian, and Bryce Slesser; Nancy Basford; Debbie Cook; Cary and Dani Barfield; and Lynn and Frank Baker.

My furry companions—Hannah, Belle, and Zan—have been my longstanding writing partners since graduate school. Their willingness to cuddle and comfort gave me much-needed breaks from writing both then and now. Hannah died in March 2016 before I finished this series of essays, before I even decided that this project should become a book. Her absence from under my desk and my life is one that I still feel every day. She was the witness to all of my most important transitions, and I was the witness to her last. She was a good dog, which was more than I could have asked of her.

Chris, Kara, and Ethan Baker deserve all of thanks for being patient with me as I wrote while being a partner and mother.

By constantly reminding me of all the possibilities, Kara helped me clarify what I want to be when I grow up. Her enthusiasm for my writing seems limitless and remarkable. My fierce oldest kiddo leaves love notes on my writing desk and gives the best hugs. I try to remind her that we don't have to figure everything out right now, and that's okay. It's a lesson we are both learning together.

I wrote "Grace Period" before Ethan was born, but the essay was published two months after his arrival. From his earliest days until he started preschool, he's been my consistent writing buddy. I wrote many of the essays in this collection with him sleeping on my chest, then sitting in my lap, then playing on the floor nearby, and now, running into my office to "help" me write. He was the witness to this transition, and he won't remember a moment of it. But I will. Thank you, Kara and Ethan, for providing the best distractions and letting me share in your joy.

I'm not sure how I can even begin to thank Chris Baker, but I will try to anyway. We've been married 15 years, and he's still the best partner and friend that I could ever hope for. When I first told him that I was ready to quit my job and take time off, he didn't hesitate or try to convince me that it was bad idea. Instead, he supported my decision unflinchingly. More than that, Chris supported me in every step of our journey with humor, love, and righteous indignation. I couldn't have built the life I have now without him; it simply wouldn't have been possible. Thank you, Chris, for being my partner in this journey and making my life better than I could have imagined. Chris, this book is dedicated to you, only you, with love and gratitude.

ABOUT THE AUTHOR

Kelly J. Baker is a freelance writer with a religious studies PhD who covers religion, racism, higher education, gender, labor, motherhood, and popular culture. She's written for *The New York Times, The Atlantic, The Rumpus, Chronicle Vitae, Religion & Politics, Killing the Buddha,* and *The Washington Post* among others.

She's the author of an award-winning book, *Gospel According to the Klan: The KKK's Appeal to Protestant America, 1915-1930* (University Press of Kansas, 2011) and *The Zombies Are Coming!: The Realities of the Zombie Apocalypse in American Culture* (Bondfire Books, 2013). Her newest book is *Grace Period: A Memoir in Pieces* (killing the buddha and Raven Books, 2017).

She's also the editor of *Women in Higher Education,* a feminist newsletter, in its 26th year, with the continued goal "to enlighten, encourage, empower and enrage women on campus."

When she's not writing assignments, editing, or wrangling two children, a couch dog, and a mean kitty, she's writing about zombie apocalypses and their discontents for the University Press of Kansas and slowly making her way toward a collections of essays about endings and other apocalypses.

Stay in touch with Kelly via her TinyLetter:
tinyletter.com/kellyjbaker

www.kellyjbaker.com

Made in the USA
San Bernardino, CA
12 December 2017